Romans

A Reasoned Defense of the Gospel

Dr. Harold A. Kime

DEDICATION

To my students, who have motivated my study and encouraged me to transform my class notes into a volume that can benefit both those in the classroom and those in ministry who desire to know God's Word and share that knowledge to the world.

PREFACE

This book is the result of many years of study and thought as I prepared lectures and class notes for teaching Romans at Lancaster Bible College. My goal is to explain the purpose and the overall structure and argument developed by Paul in this letter to the church at Rome.

Many good commentaries exist on the Epistle to the Romans and one wonders if another is needed. For this reason, I have resisted adding to that number. However, I am comforted by the words of saint Luke in the preface to his Gospel, that though many had undertaken the task of writing a gospel, he felt it prudent to record the results of his own investigation for the sake of Theophilus, his pupil. So, I offer this commentary in response to many of my students who have encouraged me to do so and in hopes that the many others who read it may through their reading join the ranks of those dear students who are my hope and joy and crown of rejoicing before our Lord Jesus at his coming.

Harold A. Kime
July, 2017

CONTENTS

Introductory Material

Introduction

Paul's letter to the Romans is the capstone of his writings. The letter is a reasoned defense of his most basic theological proposition, namely that one gains a righteous standing with God by faith, not by any works of law. The opening eleven chapters present Paul's theology in a more systematic way than any other of his letters. He argues for the sufficiency of faith in Christ's redeeming work and the deficiency of human effort in gaining righteousness by the law.

Founding of the Church at Rome

Peter. Neither Acts nor the epistles indicate how the church at Rome was founded. Paul had never visited the church (Rom. 1:10), so he could not have been its founder. Though Roman Catholic tradition suggests that Peter founded the church, several observations suggest otherwise. Paul makes no mention of Peter in Romans. It is unlikely that Paul would fail to mention Peter when he greets so many others (Rom. 16:1-16). In the early years of the church, Acts describes Peter as ministering in Palestine. Though Peter did visit Syrian Antioch (Gal. 2:11) and may have traveled as far as Corinth (1 Cor.1:10), there is no reason to believe that he journeyed to the western part of the Empire prior to Paul's writing of Romans.

Early Jewish Converts. One theory suggests that the church was founded by Jewish pilgrims to Jerusalem who were converted on the day of Pentecost (Acts 2:10). If this were the case, the church in Rome would have been well established by the time of Paul's first missionary journey.

According to the Roman historian, Suetonius, Claudius banished Jews from Rome in AD 49 because there had been rioting at the instigation of one called Chrestus. If this refers to Christ, as certainly it seems, then we can understand that riots between Jewish Christians and jealous Jews, similar to those described in Acts (Acts 13:50, 14:2, 14:19, 17:5, 17:13), led Claudius to banish both groups from the city. Aquila and Priscilla, Paul's coworkers during his 2nd and 3rd missionary journeys were part of this group (Acts 18:2). When Paul wrote Romans, they were back in Rome and intimately involved with the church, having a cell group in their own home (Rom. 16:3-5).

Paul's Influence. By the time Paul wrote to the church, the church was well established with a strong reputation (Rom. 1:8) with many workers (Rom. 16:3-16). The greetings in Romans 16 have caused some to speculate that the chapter was not originally part of the letter, but part of a greeting from a letter sent to the church at Ephesus. This conclusion is based on two observations. First, it is hard to explain how Paul was familiar with so many people at a church that he never visited. Second, Paul greeted Aquila and Priscilla whom Paul had left in Ephesus. However, these observations can be explained. Though Paul had never visited the church, he most likely had much contact with it during his 2nd and 3rd journeys. It was customary for Paul to send representatives to various locations (2 Tim. 4:10-12). The fact that Aquila and Priscilla were from Rome (Acts 18:2) would make it natural for Paul to learn about this church. That Aquila and Priscilla were in Rome when Paul wrote Romans also makes sense. Paul dropped off Aquila and Priscilla in Ephesus (Acts 18:18-26) to prepare for his 3rd journey, which would target Ephesus and Asia (Acts 19:1-10). They were his lead team. Since Paul planned on visiting Rome and Spain on a 4th journey (Rom. 15:23-24), he may have sent the team to Rome to prepare for his visit there also.

Date and Place of Writing Romans

Paul most likely wrote Romans from Corinth in AD 57 during his 3-month stay in Greece (Acts 20:2-3) at the end of his 3rd missionary journey. Several observations from Romans support this conclusion. First, the relief offering mentioned in 1 & 2 Corinthians was now complete (1 Cor. 16:1-4, 2 Cor. 8:1-7, Rom. 15:26-27). Second, the letter was delivered by Phoebe, a member of the church at Cenchrea, the eastern harbor port of Corinth (Rom. 16:1). Finally, Paul was on his way to Jerusalem (Rom. 15:25). After leaving Corinth, Paul not wanting to delay (Acts 20:16) traveled quickly to Jerusalem. It seems unlikely that Paul would have had the time to compose such an extensive letter on his hasty trip to Jerusalem. It would also make no sense to travel east before sending a letter to the west.

Identification of the Readers

The fact that the epistle is addressed to the saints at Rome (Rom. 1:7) does not answer all the questions about the original recipients. Was the church mainly Jewish, Gentile, or a balanced mix? Were all the Roman Christians the focus audience or was some subset the major focus? The banishment of Jews from Rome under Claudius in AD 49 would have resulted in the church becoming predominantly Gentile. However, this banishment would not have lasted long and certainly would have ended by the time of Claudius' death in AD 54. When Paul arrived in Rome in AD 60 the Jewish community was thriving (Acts 28:17-23). So, it is probable that many Jewish Christians would also have returned to the city. This is confirmed by Paul's greeting to several Jewish Christians at the end of Romans (Rom. 16:3-7). Additionally, the controversy over religious observances and dietary regulations (Rom. 14:1-15:13) seems clearly to be a Jewish/Gentile controversy (Rom. 15:7-12). Yet, the majority of those greeted in Romans 16 were Gentiles. So, we can conclude that the majority of those in the church were Gentile but that a minority Jewish element did exist.

In several instances Paul clearly focuses on one particular group within the church. He makes direct reference to Gentiles as his audience (Rom. 1:5-6, Rom. 1:13, Rom. 11:13). At other times, he directly addresses a Jewish group (Rom. 7:1). Though the direct address to a Jewish interlocutor (Rom. 2:17) does not refer to a member of the church, the material in chapter two would be more relevant to the Jewish Christian reader.

Occasion and Purpose for Writing

The question of why Paul wrote Romans has no simple answer. Some of the answer focuses on Paul and his situation. Other parts of the answer focus on the Romans and their situation. Still other parts focus on the broader situation of the early church.

Paul's Situation. Those who stress Paul's situation often see the letter as an introduction to the Romans with an appeal for support for a ministry in Spain. Paul had never visited the church (Rom. 1:13). He apologized for not having come before and affirmed his care and concern in spite of his absence (Rom. 1:8-15). When Paul wrote, he was completing his 3rd missionary journey and was planning a 4th journey to Spain (Rom. 15:22-24) after he delivered a relief offering to Jerusalem (Rom. 15:25-29). His desire was to visit Rome and have the church there support his ministry in Spain (Rom. 15:24). Though all this is true, it does not adequately account for the majority of material in the letter. Also, the extensive list of those greeted in chapter 16 suggests that Paul did not need an introduction; he was well known by many.

Others who stress Paul's situation often see the letter as a testament to the church in case of his death. Paul was well aware that he faced great danger in returning to Jerusalem. As he traveled back to Jerusalem, many warned about the dangers and even begged him not to go (Acts 20:22-24, Acts 21:4, Acts 21:10-23). He even asked the Romans to pray for his safety (Rom. 15:30-32). In light of this, some suggest that Paul wanted to ensure that the churches would have a reasoned statement of his teachings. Certainly, this

would account for the fact that much in Romans 1-11 seems universal in
scope with few particulars addressing the Romans' situation. However,
even if this is the case, it is clear that Paul does not address all aspects of his
theology. For example, there is little Christology in Romans. The emphasis
is on anthropology and soteriology. Paul also sets his treatise in the context
of Judaism and the Law. Of the 78 occurrences of 'law' in Romans, 76
occur in the treatise unit, Rom. 1:16-11:36, and of the 45 occurrences of the
cognates for justification (*dikaioō, dikaiosunē, dikaios*), 44 occur in the same
section. Clearly Paul is setting forth his teaching within an historical
context that is broader than his own personal situation. Finally, this
approach does not answer the question why such a testament would be sent
to the church at Rome.

Situation of the Church at Rome. Some suggest that the purpose for
writing was to address a particular situation existing in the church at Rome.
They suggest that the church was polarized along Jewish/Gentile lines with
the Jewish element taking the opinion that Gentiles should observe the
Jewish ritual and dietary restrictions found in the Law, and with the Gentile
elements taking the opinion that those who do so are weak spiritually. The
situation is drawn from Paul's instructions in Rom. 14:1-15:13. Those who
hold this position suggest that the church met in separate house churches
that were populated along ethnic lines (Rom. 16:5, Rom. 16:10-11). So,
Paul wrote Romans to correct this situation. Yet, if this is the case, one
wonders why there is so little direct mention of the situation. It is unlike
Paul to be so subtle. As Paul's letter to the Galatians attests, Paul is quick
to rebuke such ideas and quick to identify errors. Unlike his harsh rebuke
that begins Galatians, Paul is quite complementary to the Romans (Rom.
1:8). So, though this understanding of the purpose may explain why the
letter was sent to Rome, it fails to explain why the local situation is not
alluded to more often and why the major treatise unit (Rom. 1:16-11:36) is
so universal in scope.

Situation of the Early Church. It seems better to see the purpose as
addressing a broader theological controversy that existed in Paul's day.

This controversy surfaced in Acts 15 when a certain Jewish faction in the church demanded that Gentile converts should be circumcised to be saved (Acts 15:1). Though the Jerusalem council of Acts 15 decided against this teaching, the problem did not end. These Judaizers continued to spread their teaching and became a cohesive movement, the party of the concision (Gal. 2:12). They infected the church of Antioch (Gal. 2:12-13), the churches of Galatia (Gal. 5:2-3), and the church of Corinth (2 Cor. 11:13-23) with their teachings. Several years after writing Romans, they were active in Philippi (Phil. 3:2-11), and they may well have had some influence in Rome (Rom. 16:17-18). It seems they consisted mainly of Hebraists centered in Jerusalem who claimed to follow the teachings of James (Gal. 2:12). Paul wrote Romans to refute their position and persuade his readers that both Jews and Gentiles are saved by faith alone apart from any works of the Law. As such, Romans is not a systematic presentation of theological truth, but a reasoned defense of the central doctrine of the gospel -- justification by faith -- in opposition to the Judaizers' teaching that justification is by the works of the Law. See the discussion at Rom. 1:16-17 for a statement of Paul's proposition and the antithetical proposition of the Judaizers.

Genre and Rhetorical Style

Romans is an epistle that in many ways conforms to the style of a personal letter. It includes an opening salutation (Rom. 1:1-7), cordialities (Rom. 1:8-15), personal notes (Rom. 15:14-33), and closing greetings (Rom. 16:1-23). These are common to Greco-Roman personal letters of the time. However, the bulk of the content is not typical of personal letters but rather seems to follow the convention of a public treatise (Rom. 1:16-11:36). In addition, Paul employs exhortations that are similar to paraenetic letters. These distinct genres reveal the overall structure of the book.

One important type of rhetorical style used extensively in the treatise section (Rom. 1:16-11:36) is called diatribe. Diatribe is a highly emotive rhetorical style often used in lectures in which the orator or writer enters into a fictitious dialogue or debate with an opponent. It includes the following features:

- An interlocutor - the fictitious opponent addressed by means of apostrophe
- Rhetorical questions - used to introduce the interlocutor's objections and rebuttals
- The expression, *me ginoito* (may it never be!) - used to reject the interlocutor's propositions
- Emotive language – the use of more emotional and dramatic language that would be more typical of a personal confrontation
- Argumentation - various classical argument forms are incorporated to argue a point

Argument and Structure

Macro Structure. All generally agree upon the overall structure of Romans. The letter begins in the manner of traditional Greco-Romans epistles (Rom. 1:1-15), including a salutation and thanksgiving. The first major section is logical and forms the major treatise (Rom. 1:16-11:36). This is followed by a series of exhortations that follow the general form of paraenetic letters of the period (Rom. 12:1-15:13). Finally, the letter ends like traditional Greco-Roman letters with personal notes and closing greetings (Rom. 15:14-16:27). A general outline of the macro structure is as follows:

Epistolary Introduction	1:1-15
Logical Treatise	1:16-11:36
Paraenetic Epistolary Unit	12:1-15:13
Epistolary Closing	15:14-16:27

Structure of the Logical Treatise. The structure of the treatise section is also generally agreed upon. Most scholars divide the treatise into the following units: Rom. 1:16-17, Rom. 1:18-3:20, Rom. 3:21-5:21, Rom. 6:1-8:39, and Rom. 9:1-11:36. The only minor disagreement is the placement of 5:1-21. Some more recent scholars put chapter 5 with chapters 6-8.

There is much more disagreement as to the argument of the treatise and how the units fit together. Most see Paul presenting his material topically, much like a systematic theology. The normal topics include: Statement of Thesis (Rom. 1:16-17), Universal Condemnation (Rom. 1:18-3:20), Justification by Faith (Rom. 3:21-5:21), Sanctification of Believers (Rom. 6:1-8:39), and Vindication of Israel (Rom. 9:1-11:36). However, this approach seems too simple of an explanation. It fails to account for the more apologetic and polemic style of the treatise, Paul's employment of diatribe and debate, the extensive reference to Judaism and the Law, the fairly even distribution of terms related to justification throughout the treatise, and the extensive use of argumentation (claims and support).

A better approach is to see the treatise as a grand defense in the form of a debate (diatribe) between Paul and an interlocutor. At times Paul argues for his proposition; at times, he argues against his opponent's assumptions; and at other times he handles objections raised to his proposition by his opponent. Often these objections are posed in the form of rhetorical questions as in Rom. 6:1. Throughout, Paul uses Scripture as the key support for his claims. A general outline of the macro structure, following this approach would be:

Statement of Thesis.. 1:16-17
Refuting Jewish Superiority and Hope 1:18-3:20
Supporting the Alternative of Justification by Faith 3:21-4:25
Answering the Sufficiency Objection 5:1-21
Answering the Antinomian Objection...................... 6:1-8:39
Answering the Jewish Covenantal Objection 9:1-11:36

This is the approach taken in this commentary and developed in the outline that follows.

Outline

Commentary

Salutation and Opening Prayer   *1:1-15*

Summary   Paul greets the saints at Rome and expresses his prayerful desire to see them.

Structural Layout

Paul,
> bond-servant, apostle
> set apart for the gospel of God,
>> concerning His Son
to beloved in Rome
Grace and peace

I thank my God for you
> making request… in coming to you
I long to see you

Overview

The epistle begins with an introduction much like Greco-Roman letters of the day with an opening salutation and personal cordialities in the form of a thanksgiving. What is most important is to note the embellishments and additions that Paul provides. In the salutation Paul provides a major addition concerning the gospel and concerning the person of Jesus Christ. In the thanksgiving Paul provides an apology for his delay in visiting the Romans and affirms his care and concern for them.

Salutation   *1:1-7*

¹ Paul, a bond-servant of Christ Jesus, called as an apostle, set apart for the gospel of God, ² which He promised beforehand through His prophets in the holy Scriptures, ³ concerning His Son, who was born of a descendant of David according to the flesh, ⁴ who was declared the Son of God with power by the resurrection from the dead, according to the Spirit of holiness, Jesus Christ our Lord, [5] *through whom we have received grace and apostleship to bring about the obedience of faith among all the Gentiles for His name's sake,* [6] *among whom you also are the called of Jesus Christ;*

[7] *to all who are beloved of God in Rome, called as saints:*

Grace to you and peace from God our Father and the Lord Jesus Christ.

Summary   Paul greets the church at Rome emphasizing his apostolic office and the gospel of Christ, God's Son.

Structural Layout

Paul
> called apostle
> set apart for gospel
>> promised beforehand in Scriptures
>> concerning His Son
>>> seed of David
>>> Son of God
>>> Jesus Christ, Our Lord
>
> received apostleship

To all in Rome
> beloved of God
> called saints

Grace to you and peace

1:1-7 Commentary

Letters in the New Testament period begin with a formal salutation composed of three parts: identification of the writer, identification of the recipients, and the greeting. Those that are merely formal contain only the necessary facts (Acts 23:26). Expansions of any sort in the salutation are extremely important, often reflecting the author's feelings, relationships, or purposes.

Paul makes several expansions where he identifies himself as the writer (Rom. 1:1-6). He describes himself in three ways (Rom. 1:1): first, as a *bond-servant*, a term that emphasizes his humility, next as an *apostle*, a term that emphasizes his authority, and finally as *separated unto the gospel*, a phrase emphasizing his integrity and introducing the gospel as a key concept.

Next, he describes the *gospel* (Rom. 1:2), a hint concerning the purpose of the letter. The message of the gospel becomes a central focus of Paul's treatise (Rom. 1:16-17). It is not a new message, but is witnessed to in the Old Testament (Rom. 3:21). Paul understood the gospel to be the correct understanding of Judaism and its ultimate fulfillment (Acts 23:6, Acts 24:13-15, Acts 26:6-7). So, it was important for Paul to tie the gospel message to the Old Testament. This explains his extensive use of the Old Testament in Romans. Paul consistently supports his claims about the gospel by quoting from the Old Testament.

He also describes Jesus Christ (Rom. 1:3-4), the central figure in the gospel. He is the *descendant of David according to the flesh* showing that he is both human and royalty. He can aptly claim to be the Christ, the son of David (Matt. 1:1). He is also *the Son of God*, not only a man but divine. Jesus claimed to be the Son of God (Luke 22:70, Jn. 10:36) but ultimately it was the resurrection that demonstrated that this claim was true. So, He is rightfully described as *Jesus Christ, Our Lord*. Apart from this description, there is very little Christology in Romans. The letter does not develop who Jesus is but rather what Jesus has done. Yet, Paul's brief comments concerning who Jesus is indicate that an understanding of the person of Jesus is foundational to any discussion of the work of Jesus.

After describing Jesus, Paul returns to a discussion of his apostleship (Rom. 1:5-6). He describes himself as an apostle to the Gentiles (Rom. 1:5) and identifies the Romans as being within the scope of this ministry (Rom. 1:6). The expression, *obedience of faith* in 1:5 is a clear hint about Paul's thesis. The NIV rightly translates this as *obedience which comes from faith*. Compare Rom. 15:18 and Rom. 16:26. One's ability to meet God's righteous standard does not come from self-effort but from divine grace that is accessed by faith. The expression, *among whom you*, suggests that the majority of the Romans were Gentile. See comments in the Introductory Materials about the identification of the readers.

Opening Thanksgiving and Prayer   *1:8-15*

⁸*First, I thank my God through Jesus Christ for you all, because your faith is being proclaimed throughout the whole world.* ⁹*For God, whom I serve in my spirit in the preaching of the gospel of His Son, is my witness as to how unceasingly I make mention of you,* ¹⁰*always in my prayers making request, if perhaps now at last by the will of God I may succeed in coming to you.* ¹¹*For I long to see you so that I may impart some spiritual gift to you, that you may be established;* ¹²*that is, that I may be encouraged together with you while among you, each of us by the other's faith, both yours and mine.* ¹³*I do not want you to be unaware, brethren, that often I have planned to come to you (and have been prevented so far) so that I may obtain some fruit among you also, even as among the rest of the Gentiles.* ¹⁴*I am under obligation both to Greeks and to barbarians, both to the wise and to the foolish.* ¹⁵*So, for my part, I am eager to preach the gospel to you also who are in Rome.*

Summary   Paul thanks God for the Romans and prays that God will soon allow him to visit and minister to them, thus expressing his love and concern.

Structural Layout

I   thank God for you
I   make mention of you
I   long to see you
I   planned to come
      that I may impart some spiritual gift
        I may be encouraged by your faith
        I might obtain fruit
I   am under obligation
      thus
I am eager to preach the gospel

1:8-15 Commentary

Paul normally begins his letters with a word of encouragement to build a positive relationship with the readers. This was easy to do with the Romans because they had such a strong testimony of faith (Rom. 1:8). However, Paul had not yet visited this church though it seems he had been given many invitations. Does he really care? He writes to assure them of his concern in spite of his continued absence. He reveals his love through his prayers (Rom.

1:9-10) for them and his earnest desire to visit them and minister among them (Rom. 1:11-12). Note the emotion expressed in the words, *I long to see you* (Rom. 1:11). Any failure to visit was not due to his lack of concern or care for the church. He was prevented only by the situations imposed by his ministry in Asia.

His goals in coming are well balanced including both the edification of the saints: *so that I may impart some spiritual gift that you may be established* (Rom. 1:11) and the evangelism of the community: *so that I may obtain some fruit* (Rom. 1:13) and *eager to preach* (Rom. 1:15). Paul's life exemplifies the balance that the church must have. He was both a great missionary statesman and a great theologian and teacher.

Yet, Paul was never assuming. He realized that when the church gathers there must be mutual encouragement (Rom. 1:12) *each of us by the other's faith.* Everybody has something to offer. Paul associates faith with spiritual gifts (Rom. 12:3). This may be the reason for mentioning faith in Rom. 1:12. Encouragement through the exercise of spiritual gifts in the body is the responsibility of the whole congregation (Heb. 10:25).

By the expression, *impart some spiritual gift* (Rom. 1:11), Paul does not mean that he would give to them some charismatic ability but rather that the exercise of his gifts would bring blessing to them (a gift). Several observations support this conclusion. First, the *you* is plural referring to the whole church, yet according to 1 Cor. 12:29-30 no gift is for all. Second, his goal, *to establish you* best fits the idea of imparting knowledge to them, not supernatural abilities. Finally, according to 1 Cor. 12:11 gifts are distributed by the Holy Spirit, not by men.

Treatise on Justification by Faith   *1:16-11:36*

Summary   Righteousness from God by faith in Jesus Christ's sacrificial death and apart from the Law is the only means of salvation for both Jews and Gentiles.

Structural Layout

    I am not ashamed of the gospel,
        For in it the righteousness of God is revealed
            from faith to faith;

    They are without excuse.
    You are without excuse storing up wrath.
    Are we better than they?
    Not at all
    We have charged that all under sin
        Jew and Greeks
        None righteous, not one

    the righteousness of God has been manifested,
    the righteousness of God through faith in Jesus
    Abraham believed God and was reckoned as righteousness

        having been justified by faith
      we also exult in our tribulations
    Much more
        having now been justified by His blood,
      we shall be saved

        if by the transgression of the one,
      death reigned through the one,
    much more
      those who receive of the gift of righteousness will reign in life
        through the One, Jesus Christ.

    Shall we continue in sin that grace might increase?
      Died to sin, no longer slave
      Released from Law
      Spirit of life has set us free

    It is not as though the Word of God failed
      Not all Israel who are descended from Israel
      Israel did not arrive, stumbled, did not heed,
        a disobedient and obstinate people

    God has not rejected His people, has He?
      There is a remnant according to God's choice
      All Israel will be saved.

Overview

This section forms the main doctrinal part of the letter. It is a grand argument for the justification by faith that is revealed in the gospel. This is in response to the error of justification by works that is revealed in the Law. The section is not merely didactic (a teaching), but is apologetic (a defense), and even somewhat polemic (a refutation). See Appendix A for details on justification in Romans.

The main proposition presented in Rom. 1:16-17 is that righteousness is gained from God by faith in the gospel message. This proposition was opposed by the Jewish community, which claimed that righteousness was gained by works of the Law through self-effort. This debate gripped the early church as it wrestled with the nature of the gospel and the place of Gentiles in the community of faith. The individuals within the church that opposed Paul's teaching are called Judaizers. They recognized Jesus as their Messiah, but claimed that faith in the Messiah must be coupled with observance of the Law in order to be saved (Acts 15:1, Gal. 5:2, Gal. 6:12-13).

The material in Romans 1:18-11:36 is supporting material that argues in favor of the main proposition. Paul uses of Old Testament quotations at key points to prove his claims. One should also notice Paul's rhetorical style. He writes as though a debate is taking place. He uses apostrophe to speak directly to his fictional opponent or interlocutor. He also uses rhetorical questions to introduce his opponents' objections. This is a good example of classical diatribe.

Thesis: The Gospel Reveals a Righteousness from God by Faith. *1:16-17*

[16]*For I am not ashamed of the gospel, for it is the power of God for salvation to everyone who believes, to the Jew first and also to the Greek.* [17]*For in it the righteousness of God is revealed from faith to faith; as it is written, "But the righteous man shall live by faith."*

Summary   Paul is not ashamed of the gospel because it has the power to save those who believe since it reveals how to gain righteousness from God.

Structural Layout

> I am not ashamed of gospel,
> > for
> > > it is power of God for salvation
> > > to everyone who believes,
> > > > Jew first, also Greek.
> > > for
> > > > in it the righteousness of God is revealed
> > > > from faith to faith.
> > > > "the just shall live by faith"

1:16-17 Commentary

In this section Paul states the proposition that he will argue for in the rest of the treatise. The key expression is *in it the righteousness of God is revealed from faith to faith.* Paul is not talking about the righteous character of God, but a righteousness that God gives to those who believe. This is clear from Paul's use of this expression in Rom. 3:21-22. There he states that this righteousness is gained through faith in Jesus Christ. This can also be seen in Paul's use of the verb, justify (δικαιοω), which means to declare righteous (Rom. 3:24, 3:28, 5:1). The debate that Paul will deal with centers around the question, "How does a person gain righteousness?" Paul's opponents propose that righteousness is gained from self-effort by doing what the Law commands. Paul proposes that righteousness is gained from God by believing the gospel message. The two theses can be stated as follows:

Paul's Thesis   Righteousness is from God by faith in the gospel.

Opposing Thesis   Righteousness is from man by works of the Law.

The implication of both claims is that righteousness is God's requirement for gaining eternal life. Other passages support this conclusion (Ps. 94:15, Isa. 62:1, Ezek. 18:5, Ezek. 33:12-19, Matt. 5:20, Mat.t 25:46, 1 Cor. 1:30; Rom. 2:26, Rom. 5:21, Rom. 10:10; Heb. 12:14,1 Pet. 4:18).

Yet, not all that is called righteousness is true righteousness (Isa. 64:6, Ezek. 33:12-13, Matt. 5:20, Lk. 18:10). True righteousness requires perfection (Matt. 5:48, Ezek. 33:12-13). Thus, even the Old Testament prophets declared that true righteousness must be a gift given by God (Isa. 46:13, Isa. 51:5, Isa. 54:17; Jer. 23:6, Jer. 33:16, Jer. 51:10; Hos. 10:12).

This grace-righteousness is received by faith (Hab. 2:14). Paul cites the passage here in Romans and also in Galatians 3:11. In both passages, he relates Habakkuk 2:4 to the acquisition of righteousness. One gains righteousness by faith. The original sense as found in Habakkuk and quoted in Heb. 10:38 seems more directed to the trust that one who is already righteous must express in God. Yet, Paul's application of Habakkuk is not invalid. For, both the introduction and ongoing life of the righteous person must be by faith. The expression, *from faith to faith* (1:17) is added to emphasize this point. It is faith, faith, and nothing but faith that is God's requirement for gaining this righteousness. It is available to all, both Jews and Gentiles. This is a critical point within the claim. The Judaizers did not reject the idea of faith. They, however, limited its effectiveness to Jews. Faith in the Messiah was only meaningful if you kept the Law, and that meant become a proselyte and being circumcised. This salvation is for *Jews first*, not because they are more privileged, but because this is the design of God. In Rom. 2:9, judgment is also to the Jew first.

Refuting Jewish Superiority and Hope   1:18-3:20

Summary Jews do not have a superior position before God through the Law since they are sinners like the Gentiles and thus under the wrath of an impartial God.

Structural Layout

> Wrath of God is revealed against all ungodliness
> > they are without excuse
> > they knew God…exchanged the glory of God for images
>
> Therefore
> > You are without excuse
> > you practice the same things
> > you are storing up wrath
> > You bear the name Jew
> > your circumcision has become uncircumcision
>
> What then
> > Are we better than they?
> > Not at all;
> > for we have already charged that both Jews and Greeks are all under sin

Overview

This section is not merely a statement of universal sin. It is a refutation of the Jews reliance on their covenantal position with God to save them from their own sins. First, Paul describes the wrath of God upon the Gentiles because of their sin (Rom. 1:18-32). This section exhibits pronominal cohesion with the repetition of *they* and *them*. Then, he demonstrates that the Jews are in the same situation (2:1-3:8). This section exhibits pronominal cohesion with the repetition of *you*. The cohesion between these two sections is seen in the collocation of words and phrases found in each section: *practice such things*, *without excuse*, and *wrath*. Both groups have sinned, are without excuse, and under the wrath of God. The key to understanding the relationship is to observe Paul's conclusion in Rom. 3:9-20. *What then? Are we* (Jews) *better* (in our relationship with God) *than they* (Gentiles)? No. The conclusion is not simply that both groups are condemned, but that the Jews do not have an advantage.

The *therefore* at Rom. 2:1 is difficult to explain. It indicates that Jewish condemnation logically follows from the statement about Gentile condemnation in 1:18-32. But how? Some view the argument as a syllogism with 1:18-32 as the major premise about universal sinfulness. However, this approach does not explain all the material found in 2:1-3:8. It is better to view the argument as an analogy. Since the Jews are just like the Gentiles, they face the same result. This better explains why Paul refutes the differences that the Jews might claim, namely that God would judge them differently, that they have the Law, that they are circumcised and that they have many advantages.

Since none of these supposed differences refute the analogy, the conclusion (3:9-20) naturally follows. Jews are not better. They are just as much under the condemnation of sin. Thus, any attempts at gaining righteousness through the Law are doomed. The Law can only condemn (Rom. 3:19-20).

Gentile Sin and Condemnation Stated   1:18-32

[18]For the wrath of God is revealed from heaven against all ungodliness and unrighteousness of men who suppress the truth in unrighteousness, [19]because that which is known about God is evident within them; for God made it evident to them. [20]For since the creation of the world His invisible attributes, His eternal power and divine nature, have been clearly seen, being understood through what has been made, so that they are without excuse. [21]For even though they knew God, they did not honor Him as God or give thanks, but they became futile in their speculations, and their foolish heart was darkened. [22]Professing to be wise, they became fools, [23]and exchanged the glory of the incorruptible God for an image in the form of corruptible man and of birds and four-footed animals and crawling creatures.

[24]Therefore God gave them over in the lusts of their hearts to impurity, so that their bodies would be dishonored among them. [25]For they exchanged the truth of God for a lie, and worshiped and served the creature rather than the Creator, who is blessed forever. Amen.

[26]For this reason God gave them over to degrading passions; for their women exchanged the natural function for that which is unnatural, [27]and in the same way also the men abandoned the natural function of the woman and burned in their desire toward one another, men with men committing indecent acts and receiving in their own persons the due penalty of their error.

[28]And just as they did not see fit to acknowledge God any longer, God gave them over to a depraved mind, to do those things which are not proper, [29]being filled with all unrighteousness, wickedness, greed, evil; full of envy, murder, strife, deceit, malice; they

*are gossips, *[30]*slanderers, haters of God, insolent, arrogant, boastful, inventors of evil, disobedient to parents, *[31]*without understanding, untrustworthy, unloving, unmerciful; *[32]*and although they know the ordinance of God, that those who practice such things are worthy of death, they not only do the same, but also give hearty approval to those who practice them.*

Summary   In spite of the Gentiles' original position, their sin leaves them inexcusably in a state of condemnation.

Structural Layout

For

    The Wrath of God is revealed against all ungodliness
      Because
        God is evident within (among) them
          So that they are without excuse
            For
                though they knew God
              they did not honor ...
              they exchanged glory of God for images

Therefore
    God gave them over
        to impurity
        to degrading passions
        to depraved minds

1:18-32 Commentary

The unit consists of three parts. Paul begins with the basic proposition that Gentiles are condemned, under divine wrath (Rom. 1:18). The second part explains that this wrath is due to their rejection of God (Rom. 1:19-23). Finally, the consequences of this rejection are described (Rom. 1:24-28).

1:18. In spite of the expression, *all ungodliness and unrighteousness of men* (Rom. 1:18), the descriptions that follow suggest that this is not a general description about universal sinfulness but a specific description about Gentile sin and condemnation. The unit contains common Jewish apologetic arguments against Gentiles found in Josephus and Philo. The group's rejection of God resulted in idolatry, something with which Jewish readers would not readily identify. Also, Jewish readers would not readily identify with the consequences of their rejection, debauchery of every kind. Finally, the unit is relatively short when compared with the following unit dealing with Jewish sin and condemnation. There was no need to provide extensive arguments since Paul's Jewish opponents would readily agree with his conclusions as long as it did not refer to them.

Paul uses the present tense, *apokaluptetai*, stating that God's wrath is being revealed. The emphasis is not on future wrath but on current wrath. God is angry and that anger is very much visible in the world today. Those who argue that evil in the world demonstrates that a loving all powerful God does not exist, fail to understand this point. Evil, suffering, and disaster in the world does not prove that a loving and all-powerful God does not exist. It proves that this God is very upset with us and is demonstrating that anger to us.

1:19-23. These verses explain why God is so angered. Notice the causal connectors, *because* and *for*. The reason for God's wrath is their rejection of God. This rejection is inexcusable since the knowledge of God was revealed in His creation. The phrase, *that which is known about God is evident within them*, does not refer to an inward God-consciousness. Rom. 1:20 makes it clear that Paul is talking about the revelation of God found in creation (Acts 14:7). Thus, they are *without excuse* (Rom. 1:20). Paul reiterates this in Rom. 1:21-23 by developing the spiral downward. The rejection begins modestly with a lack of thankfulness, acknowledging God for his role in the world, and then quickly degenerates even to the point of idolatry. Thus, creation is sufficient to condemn when individuals reject God. However, nothing in the passage suggests that creation is sufficient to save. The knowledge of God found in creation as is described in Psalm 19:1-6 is sufficient for a person to realize there is a God. However, once a person has rejected this God, such a knowledge cannot cure the spiritual sickness that results for such rejection.

1:24-28. Paul describes God's response to their rejection of Him with the expression; *God gave them over* (Rom. 1:24, Rom. 1:26, Rom. 1:28). God's response is a judicial response. Allowing rebellious sinners to follow their own will should be understood as punishment and may well be the intended commentary on God's wrath announced in Rom. 1:18. Certainly there will be future judgment, but even now there is hell on earth and this hell is of mankind's own making. God is not the source of this sinfulness and evil. He does, however, allow it as a means of punishment upon those who reject Him.

This response affected the whole nature of mankind. What results is the depravity of the will (*impurity*), of the emotions (*degrading passions*), and of the mind (*depraved mind*). Impurity relates to immoral sexual sins (Rom. 1:24). Such dishonoring acts were prompted by dishonoring passions (Rom. 1:26). Human feelings are affected by sin and thus cannot be offered as vindication for sinful actions. The text indicates that this is true in the case of homosexual feelings. The mind also is affected (Rom. 1:28). Human reasoning is now defective and leads to conclusions that God will not approve (1 Cor. 1:18-20).

Though some have attempted to reconcile this section with the account of the fall of mankind in Genesis, there seems to be no historical relationship. Paul deals with story of Adam's sin and the nature of imputed sin in Adam in Romans 5. In Romans 1 Paul is looking at the historical development of Gentile sin in the pagan world and sees it as the corporate outworking of original sin.

Jewish Sin and Condemnation Proven   *2:1-3:8*

Summary   In spite of your position as a Jew, your sin leaves you in a state of condemnation.

Structural Layout

> Therefore
>> You are without excuse
>>> who practice such things
>> Who (God)
>>> will render to every man according to his deeds
>>>> Jew first
>>>> Greeks also
>> But
>>> You bear the name, Jew.
>>> Do you steal, commit adultery, rob temples?
>>> Your circumcision has become uncircumcision.
>> Then what advantage?
>>> Their condemnation is just.

Overview

This section argues strongly for Jewish condemnation. In so doing, Paul must destroy Jewish hope. Jews, who were secretly doing exactly what they condemned the Gentiles for doing, expected that God would treat them differently in the judgment because of their covenantal relationship with God under Law. Such is not the case. God judges and condemns both Jews and Gentiles by the same standard—works.

Thus, this section begins to make the case against gaining righteousness through Law. Such an approach can only work if you do what the Law says. Otherwise, even Jews when they sin have no special standing with God. Their circumcision, the sign of their covenantal relationship under Law, has become uncircumcision. Their position cannot save them. They are justly condemned.

The passage moves from a general statement of their condemnation and explanation of divine judgment (Rom. 2:1-16) to the specific indictment for their sins and explanation of circumcision (Rom. 2:17-29). This is followed by a short response to the objection that such Jewish condemnation would nullify the advantages of being Jewish (Rom. 3:1-8).

Some have suggested that the first section (Rom. 2:1-16) refers to pagan moralists. However, this fails to see the pronominal cohesion in the repeated use of the singular *you* in Rom. 2:1-29. It also does not consider the lexical cohesion found within the sections. Reliance on the Jewish covenantal relationship under Law is found in all three sections. Law provides no help to those who fail to obey it (Rom. 2:12-16). Circumcision is of no benefit to those who fail to obey the Law (Rom. 2:25). In spite of Jewish covenantal advantages, Jews, who sin, are justly condemned (Rom. 3:8). This dichotomy of referents also fails to see the *inclusio* that marks off the first two sections. In Rom. 2:1 the Jew is found judging the Gentiles. By the time Paul is finished with his argument in Rom. 2:27, the Gentile is judging the Jew. This irony is lost if the Jew is not seen as the referent in Rom. 2:1-16.

General Statement of Jewish Condemnation and Divine Judgment   *2:1-16*

¹*Therefore you have no excuse, everyone of you who passes judgment, for in that which you judge another, you condemn yourself; for you who judge practice the same things.* ²*And we know that the judgment of God rightly falls upon those who practice such things.* ³*But do you suppose this, O man, when you pass judgment on those who practice such things and do the same yourself, that you will escape the judgment of God?* ⁴*Or do you think lightly of the riches of His kindness and tolerance and patience, not knowing that the kindness of God leads you to repentance?* ⁵*But because of your stubbornness and unrepentant heart you are storing up wrath for yourself in the day of wrath and revelation of the righteous judgment of God,*

⁶*who will render to each person according to his deeds:* ⁷*to those who by perseverance in doing good seek for glory and honor and immortality, eternal life;* ⁸*but to those who are selfishly ambitious and do not obey the truth, but obey unrighteousness, wrath and indignation.* ⁹*There will be tribulation and distress for every soul of man who does evil, of the Jew first and also of the Greek,* ¹⁰*but glory and honor and peace to everyone who does good, to the Jew first and also to the Greek.* ¹¹*For there is no partiality with God.*

¹²*For all who have sinned without the Law will also perish without the Law, and all who have sinned under the Law will be judged by the Law;* ¹³*for it is not the hearers of the Law who are just before God, but the doers of the Law will be justified.* ¹⁴*For when Gentiles who do not have the Law do instinctively the things of the Law, these, not having the Law, are a law to themselves,* ¹⁵*in that they show the work of the Law written in their hearts, their conscience bearing witness and their thoughts alternately*

accusing or else defending them, [16]*on the day when, according to my gospel, God will judge the secrets of men through Christ Jesus.*

Summary   Because you practice that which you condemn in others, you stand condemned, since God judges all impartially based on what they do.

Structural Layout

Therefore
you are without excuse.
> You who passes judgment
> you practice the same things.

The judgment of God falls on those who practice such things
> Do you suppose you will escape?
> Do you think lightly of the riches of kindness, forbearance, patience?
> You are storing up wrath.

Who (God) will render to every man according to his deeds
> those …doing good   eternal life
> those …do not obey   wrath
> > Jew first
> > Greek also
> For no partiality with God
> For
> > all sinned without Law perish without
> > all sinned under Law   judged by Law
> > not the hearers of Law, but doers will be justified

2:1-16 Commentary

Most English translations divide the section into two paragraphs (Rom. 2:1-11 and Rom. 2:12-16). This fits well with the grammatical structure but does not fit as well with the logical and semantic structure of the passage. I suggest another logical break between verses five and six. The NIV and NLV support this three-paragraph structure. Several structural devices suggest that a break exists between five and six. First, the pronoun, *you* found in Rom. 2:1-5, is not found in Rom. 2:6-16. Second, at Rom. 2:6 the topic shifts from the sin of the person under consideration to the impartiality of divine judgment. God becomes the subject of the verbs. Finally, the fact that the

Septuagint passage, Prov. 24:12, quoted in verse six begins with a relative pronoun explains its presence at verse six and why there is a single sentence continuing into verse six in the Greek text.

2:1-5. Starting with Rom. 2:1, the *they* that dominated Rom. 1:18-32 is replaced with the singular *you*. Who is this new person to whom Paul now directs his attention? It cannot be the Roman Christians to whom the letter is addressed. Paul in addressing the readers employs a plural you (Rom. 1:6-15). This individual is stubborn, unrepentant, and storing up wrath (Rom. 2:5), but Paul highly acclaimed the Roman Christians for their faith (Rom. 1:8). Rather Paul, using diatribe, addresses an interlocutor, a fictitious opponent.

Some suggest that the interlocutor is a pagan moralist but it is best to identify the individual as a Jew. First, the singular pronoun, *you*, is used throughout the chapter and in Rom. 2:17 it clearly refers to a Jew. Second, the issue of Law is brought up in connection with this individual (Rom. 2:12-13). Third, the description of the individual matches Paul's description of the Jews (Rom. 10:21). Finally, throughout the book Paul only has in view two groups, -- Jews and Gentiles (Rom. 1:16, Rom. 2:9, Rom. 3:9, Rom. 4:9, Rom. 9:30-31, Rom. 11:25-26). The addition of a third group would be out of place. So, Paul, using diatribe, addresses a Jewish interlocutor as a typical representative of all Jews.

Though Paul moves from a discussion that focuses on Gentiles (Rom. 1:18-32) to a discussion that focuses on Jews, he does relate the two discussions through the use of several repeated terms and phrases. Both are *without excuse* (Rom. 1:20, Rom. 2:1), *practice such things* (Rom. 1:32, Rom. 2:1-3) and are under *wrath* (Rom. 1:18, Rom. 2:5). This Jew is just like the Gentiles and therefore will experience the same wrath.

The reason for his condemnation is not that he judges others but that he practices the same sins as do those he judges. Paul's three-fold repetition of *practice such things* emphasizes Paul's point (Rom. 2:1-3). His judging is self-condemning (Rom. 2:1) since it reveals that he is aware of God's standards and that God judges based on those standards. So, when he does the very things that he judges in others, he cannot claim that his actions are excusable. He is *without excuse* (Rom. 2:1).

Yet, this Jew believed that God would not judge him as He did the Gentiles. This false hope is described in Rom. 2:3-4. He thought that affirming God's standards by judging others would be sufficient grounds for him to escape God's judgment (Rom. 2:3). Yet, affirming God's standards only served to condemn him since his judging was a clear acknowledgement of those standards. How could this Jew reason that he could violate God's standards with impunity when Gentiles could not? He reasoned that he had a special covenantal relationship with God. Paul describes this relationship with the expression *the riches of His kindness and tolerance and patience*. This false hope was first of all a misunderstanding of God's *kindness*. In the LXX, kindness—*chrēstotēs*, is used to affirm God's goodness in relationship with His covenant (Ps 24:7, Ps 144:7). It was also a misunderstanding of God's *patience* (Rom. 2:4). Did God's hesitation in punishing him indicate that he would not be punished? No! God was mercifully giving him time to repent. His failure to repent would result in wrath (Rom. 2:5).

2:6-11. This section is designed to correct the misunderstanding about God's judgment suggested by the interlocutor in Rom. 2:3-4. This Jew must understand that God will not treat him differently in the judgment than He does Gentiles. God's judgment is impartial (Rom. 2:11). The unit begins with a quotation from Prov. 24:12 (LXX), purposed to identify the standard for judgment used by God. As is typical in Romans, Paul provides Scriptural proof for major claims with which his opponent would not agree. Here the claim is that God judges all in exactly the same way. He judges *every person according to his deeds* (Rom. 2:6). This is reinforced by the repetition of *doing* in Rom. 2:6-10.

How are we to understand this emphasis on doing? It does not refer to works salvation; nor does it imply faith on the part of the person gaining eternal life. The passage makes no mention of salvation or faith. Paul is only showing that God will judge impartially based on works. The act of judging is very different from the act of saving. In judgment God gives people what they rightly deserve. In salvation God delivers people from what they deserve and gives them what they do not deserve. So, this passage is referring to God's judgment that ultimately leads to the condemnation of all (Rom. 3:9).

Rom. 2:7 describes a valid means of gaining eternal life (Matt 19:16-22, Rom. 2:13, Rom. 7:9, Rom. 8:3-4). Anyone who could live up to the standard of Law would be rewarded with eternal life. Though this method of gaining life is theoretically possible, it is practically impossible because of sin (Rom. 3:20, 8:3, Gal. 3:11-12).

Paul's point is that the Jews should not expect to be treated any differently in the judgment than the Gentiles will be treated. God is impartial in judgment. And since the Jews have sinned, just like the Gentiles, they too stand condemned. Their covenantal position as Jews does not change the situation. God treats Jews and Gentiles in the exact same way, *to the Jew first and also to the Greek* (Rom. 2:9-10). Yet, Paul is not suggesting by the word *first* any sense of partiality. The idea seems to be more temporal. The Jews were first to hear of God's salvation (Rom. 1:16) and also first to hear of His judgment.

2:12-16. In this third paragraph, Paul introduces Law into the discussion. The Jewish debater would respond that the very fact that God has given the Jews His Law and has not given it to the Gentiles would suggest that there is a difference between them and that this difference would suggest a difference in God's judgment of the two. Paul responds to this objection by affirming that the Jewish possession of the Law makes no difference with reference to divine judgment since those who sin under Law (Jews) are condemned by the Law (Rom. 2:12) and those who sin without the Law (Gentiles) are condemned by a law of conscience (Rom. 2:14-15). Thus, both have law. The Mosaic Law given to the Jews is external. The conscience given to all is internal.

The concept of an innate moral nature was commonly held throughout the Greek world and was recognized within Jewish thought. When Paul states that Gentiles *do instinctively the things of the Law* he is not eluding to Christians but to the fact that morality is universal, even among those to whom the Law

32

was not given. Since this is the case, God can apply the same standard of judgment to all.

The final explanation comes when Paul states, *it is not the hearers of the Law who are just before God, but the doers of the Law will be justified* (Rom. 2:14). The Jew understood the Law as providing an unconditional covenant by God by which he was assured of God's mercy. Paul corrects this by stating that the covenant of Law was conditioned by obedience. Those who seek a righteous standing with God by means of Law must obey it completely. In Rom. 3:20 Paul concludes that no one can ultimately gain such a standing with God by Law because all are violators of Law. Therefore, it seems clear that Paul's affirmation that the doers of the Law will be justified is only theoretical. There are no doers of the Law.

Specific Indictment of Jewish Sin and Explanation of Circumcision   *2:17-29*

[17]*But if you bear the name "Jew" and rely upon the Law and boast in God,* [18]*and know His will and approve the things that are essential, being instructed out of the Law,* [19]*and are confident that you yourself are a guide to the blind, a light to those who are in darkness,* [20]*a corrector of the foolish, a teacher of the immature, having in the Law the embodiment of knowledge and of the truth,* [21]*you, therefore, who teach another, do you not teach yourself? You who preach that one shall not steal, do you steal?* [22]*You who say that one should not commit adultery, do you commit adultery? You who abhor idols, do you rob temples?* [23]*You who boast in the Law, through your breaking the Law, do you dishonor God?* [24]*For "the name of God is blasphemed among the Gentiles because of you," just as it is written.*

[25]*For indeed circumcision is of value if you practice the Law; but if you are a transgressor of the Law, your circumcision has become uncircumcision.* [26]*So if the uncircumcised man keeps the requirements of the Law, will not his uncircumcision be regarded as circumcision?* [27]*And he who is physically uncircumcised, if he keeps the Law, will he not judge you who though having the letter of the Law and circumcision are a transgressor of the Law?* [28]*For he is not a Jew who is one outwardly, nor is circumcision that which is outward in the flesh.* [29]*But he is a Jew who is one inwardly; and circumcision is that which is of the heart, by the Spirit, not by the letter; and his praise is not from men, but from God.*

Summary   Your position as a Jew is nullified because you have broken the Law in which case circumcision provides no benefit.

Structural Layout

You bear the name Jew	know His will
rely upon Law	approve things excellent
boast in God	guide to blind
Do you not teach yourself?	
Steal?	Rob temples?
Commit adultery?	Dishonor God?

For "the name of God is blasphemed among the Gentiles because of you," just as it is written.

Circumcision is of value
    if you keep the Law
    if you are transgressor
become uncircumcision
    if uncircumcised keeps Law
be regarded as circumcised
    if he keeps the Law
he will judge you, a transgressor
He is a Jew who is one inwardly,
circumcision of the heart, by the Spirit

2:17-29 Commentary

2:17-24. Having argued that God will judge the Jews using the same standard as the Gentiles, Paul returns to his indictment of the Jews and to the diatribe style used in Rom. 2:1-5 but now he becomes more specific. Paul clearly identifies his opponent as a Jew (Rom. 2:17) and sarcastically describes his opponent's own opinion of himself (Rom. 2:17-20).

Rom. 2:17-18 describes the Jew's personal confidence in his relationship to God. He is a *Jew*, part of God's chosen people. He *relies upon the Law* in that he believes that his relationship to Law will lead to his escape from divine judgment (Rom. 2:3). He *knows God's will* and *approves the essential things being instructed out of the Law*. This knowledge of Law prompts him to judge others (Rom. 2:1) yet it does not result in his doing what the Law says (Rom. 2:13).

Rom. 2:19-20 describes the Jew's condescending attitude toward Gentiles. He sees himself as a *guide, a light, a corrector*, and *a teacher*. He views the Gentiles as *blind, in darkness, foolish*, and *immature*. Clearly, he claims a religious superiority over the Gentiles. This is exactly the attitude of Jews in Paul's day.

Paul dramatically rejects this claim, using the literary device, interrogation— a use of questions to forcefully indict. He charges his Jewish interlocutor with the very sins for which this Jew condemns the Gentiles. (Rom. 2:21-23). Yet, these are only accusations. Paul must complete the section by proving that the accusations are true. He does so by quoting from Isa. 52:5 or Ezek. 36:20 (Rom. 2:24). Isa. 52:5 is part of a grand series of deliverance speeches that describe both Jehovah and Jerusalem as awakening out of sleep and restoring past glory (Isa. 51:9-52:12). The Lord promises to deliver the captives from the oppressors who *blaspheme the name of God continually*. If Paul is alluding to this passage, he sees the blaspheme occurring due to Israel's sin that led to their captivity. God's judgment upon Israel allowed the Gentile nations to distain the God of Israel. Ezek. 36:20 is more probably the passage that Paul had in mind. The Gentiles nations *profaned My holy name* because of their sin. Israel also had *profaned His holy name among the nations* (Ezek. 36:21). So, it is clear that Israel had sinned. Paul's charge is proven true.

2:25-29. He ends the section by drawing some conclusions about his opponent's Jewish covenantal position, which he alludes to with the term, *circumcision*. Paul, employing metonymy, substitutes the concrete rite of circumcision for the abstract position of the Jew, though it is obvious that this Jew saw the two as being inseparable. Because of his sin, this Jew has forfeited the advantage of his position with God under Law. His *circumcision has become uncircumcision* (Rom. 2:25). He has no advantage over the uncircumcised Gentiles. Under Law, the promise of eternal life is directly tied to doing (Rom. 2:13). Since this is the case, anyone, even a Gentile, who did what the Law stipulated would gain this position, *his uncircumcision* would *be regarded as circumcision* (Rom. 2:26). Ironically, this Jew, who in Rom. 2:1-5 was judging the Gentiles, is now potentially judged by them (Rom. 2:27).

Paul ends the section with a clarification on what constitutes a true Jew, one who indeed had a position with God that would lead to escaping God's judgment (Rom. 2:28-29). This true Jew is one whose relationship with God is *inward, a circumcision of the heart by the Spirit*. Paul is not alluding to the New Testament Christian but to the Old Testament saints who lived under the Law. Even under Law, it was clear that a person's relationship with God must be inward, having a circumcised heart (Deut. 10:16, Deut. 30:6, Jer. 4:4). Though it is possible that Paul sees the Holy Spirit as the agent of this renewal, it is more likely that the expression, *en pneutami* does not refer to the Holy Spirit but to the individual's spirit. Such a relationship requires a new spirit (Ezek. 11:19, Ezek. 18:31, Ezek. 36:26).

Jewish Condemnation is Just 3:1-8

[1]Then what advantage has the Jew? Or what is the benefit of circumcision? [2]Great in every respect. First of all, that they were entrusted with the oracles of God. [3]What then? If some did not believe, their unbelief will not nullify the faithfulness of God, will it? [4]May it never be! Rather, let God be found true, though every man be found a liar, as it is written, "That You may be justified in Your words, And prevail when You are judged."

[5]But if our unrighteousness demonstrates the righteousness of God, what shall we say? The God who inflicts wrath is not unrighteous, is He? (I am speaking in human terms.) [6]May it never be! For otherwise, how will God judge the world? [7]But if through my lie the truth of God abounded to His glory, why am I also still being judged as a sinner? [8]And why not say (as we are slanderously reported and as some claim that we say), "Let us do evil that good may come"? Their condemnation is just.

Summary   In spite of the advantages of Judaism and the glory God receives when He judges, Jews are justly condemned.

Structural Layout

> What is the benefit of circumcision?
>> Great in every respect.
>> They were entrusted with the oracles of God
> What then?
>> Their unbelief will not nullify the faithfulness of God, will it?
>> May it never be!
>> The God who inflicts wrath is not unrighteous, is He?
>> May it never be!
> Their condemnation is just.

3:1-8 Commentary

3:1-4. At this point an objection to Jewish condemnation is raised and handled. The rhetorical questions (Rom. 3:1) are raised by the Jewish interlocutor. If because of sin Jews are no better off than Gentiles (Rom. 2:25), what is the advantage of being Jewish? Paul delays a full discussion of this issue until chapter nine. At this point he is willing to give only a partial response. He argues that, in spite of any advantage, they are justly condemned by a faithful God.

The argument may be the most difficult to follow in the whole book. He begins by stating that there are advantages to being Jewish (Rom. 3:2). The main advantage is that they were *entrusted with God's oracles*. Paul deliberately uses a general and all-inclusive term, *oracles*. These oracles include God's laws, covenants and promises.

If God has given promises to Israel, will not His judgment of Jews result in divine unfaithfulness (Rom. 3:3)? No! Paul quotes Ps. 51:4 to show that God will be found faithful in spite of Israel's unfaithfulness (Rom. 3:4).

3:5-8. This leads to a second objection from the interlocutor (Rom. 3:5). If Israel's unfaithfulness helps to demonstrate God's faithfulness—for it is harder to be faithful when others are unfaithful—should not God commend them rather than condemn them? No! This line of argument would result in turning moral judgment upside down. If God cannot judge Jews for their sins, then he could not judge Gentiles either (Rom. 3:6). They could also not judge Paul as a sinner for preaching the gospel (Rom. 3:7). This gospel that they considered a *lie* would be *abounding to God's glory*. Indeed, the ultimate moral philosophy would be to promote as much evil as possible so that God would receive even more glory (Rom. 3:8). Such a point of view is absurd and must be rejected.

Having shown his opponents argument to be absurd, Paul ends the section by affirming his own position. *Their condemnation is just.*

Conclusion: The Jew has no superior position before God   3:9-20

⁹*What then? Are we better than they? Not at all; for we have already charged that both Jews and Greeks are all under sin;*

¹⁰*as it is written,*

"There is none righteous, not even one; ¹¹There is none who understands, There is none who seeks for God; ¹²All have turned aside, together they have become useless; There is none who does good, There is not even one."

¹³*"Their throat is an open grave, With their tongues they keep deceiving,"*

"The poison of asps is under their lips";

¹⁴*"Whose mouth is full of cursing and bitterness";*

¹⁵*"Their feet are swift to shed blood, ¹⁶Destruction and misery are in their paths, ¹⁷And the path of peace they have not known."*

¹⁸*"There is no fear of God before their eyes."*

¹⁹*Now we know that whatever the Law says, it speaks to those who are under the Law, so that every mouth may be closed and all the world may become accountable to God; ²⁰because by the works of the Law no flesh will be justified in His sight; for through the Law comes the knowledge of sin.*

Summary   The Jew has no advantage over the Gentiles with respect to divine judgment since both are under sin's condemnation against which the Law affords no help.

Structural Layout

> What then?
>> Are we better than they? No!
>>> for both Jews and Greeks <u>all under sin</u>
>>>> <u>none</u> righteous, understand, seek God
>>>> <u>all</u> turned aside
>>>> <u>none</u> does good, not even one

> Law speaks
>> that every mouth stopped
>>> all the world accountable
>> for by works of Law no flesh justified

3:9-20 Commentary

In this section Paul concludes the argument begun at Rom. 1:18. His conclusion is not simply that the whole world is condemned, but rather that Jews are not superior to Gentiles and will find no saving help in the Law. He states the first part of the conclusion in Rom. 3:9, offers final scriptural support for universal sin in Rom. 3:10-18, and then draws the second part of the conclusion in Rom. 3:19-20.

3:9. The *we* in Rom. 3:9 has been understood as referring to the Roman Christians, to Paul and his associates, or to the Jews. It seems most likely that Paul is referring to the Jews but also includes himself as a Jew. Though the *we* in Rom. 3:8 is an editorial we and refers exclusively to Paul, the *we* in Rom. 3:5 must refer to the Jews for several reasons. First, the verse begins with a strong inferential question, *What then?* about superiority. No such inference can be drawn from the discussion of Paul in Rom. 3:8. Second, the use of *they* and *you* in chapters one and two referring to Gentiles and Jews parallels the *we* and *they*. Finally, the explanation that both *Jews and Greeks* are under sin suggests that the two groups are the focus of the question.

There is also some debate about the rendering of the verb, *are we better* (*proexometha*). The form is either a middle or passive form. If it is middle, it can be translated, *Do we have an advantage?* If it is passive, it should be translated, *Are we excelled?* The middle rendering is preferred by nearly all

English translations. Paul has already mentioned that Jews do have advantages (Rom. 3:1). So, the question with its negative response must refer to some specific advantage. Paul means that the Jews are not superior in righteousness and thus better off before God with respect to His judgment. This is clear from the previous discussion. The reason for this is that *Both Jews and Greeks are all under sin.* Greeks have been shown to be under sin in Rom. 1:18-32 and Jews in Rom. 2:1-2:29.

But what does Paul mean with the expression, *under sin?* Some suggest that Paul is talking about human enslavement to sin but this seems out of place in the current argument. It seems better to understand Paul as saying that all are under the indictment of sin (Gal. 3:22). All are sinners deserving nothing but divine tribulation and wrath.

3:10-18. Having stated his ultimate conclusion, Paul now sets forth a list of scriptures as overwhelming confirmation of that conclusion. The number of the quotations is notable, six passages in all (Ps. 14:1-3, Ps. 5:9, P.s 140:3, Ps. 10:7, Isa. 59:7-8, Ps. 36:1). Nowhere else in Romans does Paul provide such an extensive list. He wants to make it clear that what he has concluded is exactly what the Scriptures teach. Along with the quantity, the quotations also exhibit certain important characteristics. First, they emphasize the universal nature of sin with the words, *none* and *all,* and the phrase, *not even one.* Second, the reference to the *throat, tongues, mouth, feet,* and *eyes* suggests that the effect on the individual is total. Third, both Gentiles and Jews are the referents in these verses. The quotations from Ps 14:1-3 refers specifically to Gentiles, while Isa 59:7-8 refers specifically to Israel.

3:19-20. Paul concludes the sections by drawing implications concerning the Law. The Jews viewed the Law as a means of escaping the judgment due them because of their sins (Rom. 2:3, Rom. 2:13). They believed that their covenantal position under Law would result in God's favor in spite of their sin. Paul has demonstrated that because of their sin, they have lost any position before God that Law might afford (Rom. 2:25). Paul now restates this concept by clarifying what the Law does (Rom. 3:19) and what it does not do (Rom. 3:20) for those who are under it.

The *Law* that speaks in Rom. 3:19 must refer to the whole Old Testament. For, Paul uses the term to refer to the quotations given in Rom. 3:10-18, none of which are from the books of Moses. These Old Testament quotations about sin speak to *those who are under the Law.* This seems to refer specifically to the Jews (Rom. 2:12). Though the quotations certainly apply to the Gentiles, they have more direct application to the Jews. These quotations leave the Jews with *every mouth closed.* They have no defense against the charges. In the end, *all the world becomes accountable.*

This is true because *by the works of the Law no flesh will be justified.* Yet, in Rom. 2:13 Paul stated that *the doers of the Law will be justified.* Rom. 3:20 is not a contradiction but a clarification to that statement. Since there are no doers of the Law, the Law cannot be the source of their righteousness. Thus, sinners cannot gain righteousness through the Law. Rather, they are condemned by it (Rom. 2:25). For, the Law does not provide a remedy for sin; it simply reveals it (Rom. 7:7).

Supporting the Alternative: Justification by Faith   3:21-4:25

Summary   Justification by faith is provided by the sacrificial death of Christ, is proven scripturally in the life of Abraham, and is sufficient to overcome our sin in Adam.

Structural Layout

> Now apart from the Law
> the righteousness of God has been manifest
>   through faith in Jesus Christ
> justified as a gift
>   through redemption in Christ
>   as a propitiation
>
> What has Abraham found?
> "Abraham believed…was credited to him as righteousness."
> It was written for our sake also,
>   to whom it will be credited,
>   as those who believe in Him
>   who raised Jesus our Lord from the dead

Overview

After refuting the claim that Jews under Law are protected from divine judgment by showing that all men are under condemnation for their sins, Paul offers the alternative approach to gaining righteousness, namely that righteousness is gained by faith in Jesus Christ. He begins by explaining this alternate approach (Rom. 3:21-31) and then offers scriptural and historical proof for this approach in the life of Abraham (Rom. 4:1-25).

The section is more than a simple presentation of justification by faith. It is highly argumentative, defending as well as explaining the truth of justification by faith.

Proposition: Righteousness Gained from God By Faith in Jesus *3:21-31*

²¹*But now apart from the Law the righteousness of God has been manifested, being witnessed by the Law and the Prophets,* ²²*even the righteousness of God through faith in Jesus Christ for all those who believe; for there is no distinction;* ²³*for all have sinned and fall short of the glory of God,*

²⁴*being justified as a gift by His grace through the redemption which is in Christ Jesus;* ²⁵*whom God displayed publicly as a propitiation in His blood through faith. This was to demonstrate His righteousness, because in the forbearance of God He passed over the sins previously committed;* ²⁶*for the demonstration, I say, of His righteousness at the present time, so that He would be just and the justifier of the one who has faith in Jesus.*

²⁷*Where then is boasting? It is excluded. By what kind of law? Of works? No, but by a law of faith.* ²⁸*For we maintain that a man is justified by faith apart from works of the Law.* ²⁹*Or is God the God of Jews only? Is He not the God of Gentiles also? Yes, of Gentiles also,* ³⁰*since indeed God who will justify the circumcised by faith and the uncircumcised through faith is one.* ³¹*Do we then nullify the Law through faith? May it never be! On the contrary, we establish the Law.*

Summary   Apart from the Law, a righteousness from God by faith in Christ is available to all because of Christ's sacrificial death that frees God to justify sinners.

Structural Layout

The Righteousness of God has been manifest
    apart from the Law
    witnessed by the Law
the righteousness of God
    through faith in Jesus Christ
    for all who believe
        being justified as a gift
            through redemption in Christ
        whom God displayed as a propitiation
        to demonstrate His righteousness
                so that He would be just and justifier

Then
      Where is boasting?   What kind of Law?
      Is God of Jews only? Do we nullify Law?

3:21-31 Commentary

In this section Paul presents his alternative to gaining righteousness through the Law. He claims that righteousness is available to all through faith in Jesus Christ (Rom. 3:21-23). Yet, such a claim seems illogical. How can a righteous God simply declare as righteous those who He has already determined are unrighteous? The answer is in understanding how Jesus' death satisfied the demands of God's righteous and freed Him to declare as righteous those who believe in Jesus (Rom. 3:24-26). Paul concludes the section by suggesting the implications of this approach to gaining righteousness (Rom. 3:27-31).

3:21-23. Paul begins by presenting his alternative method of gaining righteousness (Rom. 3:21). The conjunction *But* indicates a contrast to the failed method of gaining righteousness by works of the Law (Rom. 3:20). This alternative is *apart from the Law*. It is independent of Law and thus there are no conditions of Law that must be met to gain this righteousness. Yet, this righteousness is *witnessed by the Law and the Prophets*. It is not new. Paul alluded to it in Rom. 1:2. The gospel message, namely that one gains righteousness as a gift by faith, is both promised and mentioned in the Old Testament. Yet, Paul makes it clear that this righteousness is not the same as the righteousness that is source in law. This righteousness comes from

God by faith apart from the Law. As in Rom. 1:17 *the righteousness of God* does not refer to God's character but to *a righteousness from God*. This must be the case since this righteousness is *through faith for all who believe* (Rom. 3:22). This is a righteousness that one gains as a result of believing. Though Paul might have in mind an imputed righteousness—the idea that the recipient actually becomes righteous, it is more likely that Paul refers to declared righteousness—God offers a verdict of righteousness. This is more in keeping with the meaning of the verb, *justify—dikaioō* (Rom. 3:24). This righteousness is available *for all who believe*. It is not only for Jews since *all have sinned*. All people are equally guilty and in the same condition. So, the solution must be the same for all.

3:24-26. Next Paul explains how a righteous God can declare as righteous those who clearly are not righteous. The key is the work of Jesus Christ. This work is described with two key words, *redemption* and *propitiation*.

Redemption (apolutrōsis) is the act of buying out of slavery or captivity by means of a payment or ransom (1 Cor.1:30; Eph. 1:7; Col 1:14). Sinners are both enslaved to sin (Rom. 7:14) and captives of sin (Rom. 7:23). Christ paid the ransom price (Matt. 20:28, Heb. 9:5), death, that God demands for sin (Gen. 2:17; Rom. 6:23).

The word, *propitiation (hilastērion)* is found in the NT only again in Heb. 9:5 where it refers to the mercy seat in the Tabernacle, the cover of the Ark of the Covenant. Throughout the Septuagint it refers to this mercy seat. (Ex. 25, Lev. 16). It is the place of atonement. The word for atoning sacrifice, *hilasmos*, is not used here but is found in 1 Jn. 2:2 and 1 Jn. 4:10. Clearly, Paul has in mind the Day of Atonement (Lev. 23:26-44) when the High Priest sprinkled the blood of atoning sacrifice on the mercy seat to atone for the sins of the people. Christ's death of the cross relates both to the place of atonement and the sacrifice of atonement that satisfied God's righteous demand for payment of sin. He is both the place where this atonement occurred and the sacrifice by which atonement occurred. However, under the Law the High Priest would enter the inner sanctuary alone and sprinkle the blood of the atoning sacrifice upon the mercy seat. In contrast, Christ was *displayed publicly* on a cross for all to see (Rom. 3:25). Why this public display that contrasts with the Old Testament pattern? It was necessary to *demonstrate His* (God's) *righteousness*. God, who delayed judgment for sin in the past, must be publicly vindicated. He did so justly, knowing that His Son would satisfy His righteous demand for punishment.

As a result, God can offer righteousness as a gift while at the same time remaining just. He is *just and justifier* (Rom. 3:26). He retains His righteous character and at the same time declares as righteous those unrighteous individuals who have *faith in Jesus*. In the death of Christ, a righteous God found a way to deal with human sinfulness without condemning humans to eternal death.

3:27-31. The section concludes with four implications of this approach (Rom. 3:27-31). (1) It does not allow for boasting as Law would (Rom. 3:27). Where there are works that merit a declaration of righteousness from God, there is room for self-boasting (Rom. 4:2). In contrast, faith does not result in self-boasting but rather results in boasting in God (1 Cor. 1:30-31). There is no boasting *by a law of faith*, since trusting in God begins with admitting that we are sinners and that we cannot solve our sin problem, and ends with the acknowledgement that God has done it all. (2) It does not include works (Rom. 3:28). Faith and works are mutually exclusive (Rom. 4:14, Rom11:6). (3) It is not limited to the Jews (Rom. 2:29-30). Since there is only one true God--a fundamental doctrine of Judaism, this one God must be the justifier of both groups. He *justifies the circumcised by faith and the uncircumcised through faith*. One should not make too much of a distinction between the two prepositions, *by* (*ek*) and *through* (*dia*). Both merely suggest that faith is the response needed to gain a righteous standing with God. (4) It gives the Law its rightful place (Rom. 3:31). The purpose of Law is to make sinners aware of their sinfulness (Rom. 3:19) and to drive them to look outside of themselves for help (Rom. 7:24). Justification by faith uses the Law in this way. Only when individuals understand their sinfulness will they consider the gospel. The Law becomes an important message, not because one can be justified by it, but because it alerts people to their need for deliverance.

Abraham's Experience Proof for Justification by Faith   4:1-25

Summary   Abraham's experience provide both historic and scriptural proof that people are justified by faith apart from Law.

Structural Layout

What has Abraham found?
>"Abraham believed...was credited as righteousness." Gen. 15:6

Is this blessing upon the circumcised or uncircumcised also?
>It was credited while he was uncircumcised.

The promise was to his descendants
>not through Law
>but through righteousness of faith

He believed
>in hope, without becoming weak, grew strong in faith
>therefore it was credited to him

It was written
>for our sake to whom it will be credited who believe.

Overview

Paul, desiring to support his proposition that individuals are justified by faith, turns to Scripture (Gen. 15:6) and recounts the experience of Abraham (Rom. 4:1-8), namely that he was justified by faith. This experience is not exclusively for the circumcised since Abraham's justification was before his circumcision (Rom. 4:9-12).   Though the Law was introduced later, Abraham's descendants must also gain righteousness by faith not by Law (Rom. 4:13-17).   Abraham's faith was strong and dynamic and defines the type of faith that is necessary to be justified (Rom. 4:18-22).   Since it was written as part of Scripture, we must conclude that this experience involves universal truth that is applicable to everyone since God recorded it for posterity (Rom. 4:23-25).

In the chapter Paul argues from the specific to the general.   He begins by discussing Abraham's specific experience and ends by showing that this experience is validly to be the general experience of every man.   This experience confirms that everyone must gains righteousness as a gift from God by faith without the works of the Law.

Abraham Was Justified by Faith 4:1-8

[1]What then shall we say that Abraham, our forefather according to the flesh, has found? [2]For if Abraham was justified by works, he has something to boast about, but not before God. [3]For what does the Scripture say? "Abraham believed God, and it was credited to him as righteousness." [4]Now to the one who works, his wage is not credited as a favor, but as what is due. [5]But to the one who does not work, but believes in Him who justifies the ungodly, his faith is credited as righteousness,

[6]just as David also speaks of the blessing on the man to whom God credits righteousness apart from works: [7]"Blessed are those whose lawless deeds have been forgiven, And whose sins have been covered. [8]"Blessed is the man whose sin the Lord will not take into account."

Summary   Abraham, like David, as Scripture confirms, was justified by faith, not as what was due him but as a gift.

Structural Layout

What then shall we say that Abraham, our forefather has found?
    if justified by works,
has something to boast about

what does the Scripture say?
    "Abraham believed God,
    it was credited to him as righteousness."

Now
    to the one who works,
his wage is credited as what is due.
    to the one who does not work,
his faith is credited as righteousness,

David also speaks
    "Blessed are those whose lawless deeds have been forgiven,
        And whose sins have been covered.

4:1-8 Commentary

4:1-5. Paul begins by offering scriptural support for his proposition that one gains a righteous standing with God by faith apart from the works of law. He does so by quoting God's declaration about Abraham in Gen. 15:6.

Paul asks the question, *What then shall we say that Abraham, our forefather according to the flesh, has found?* Though the question seems general, the prior context and the answer to the question itself suggest that Paul is inquiring about what Abraham discovered concerning justification.

The choice of Abraham is significant. He was the *forefather* of the nation of Israel, the one to whom Jews traced their ancestry (Matt 3:9; Luke 3:8). To demonstrate that Abraham was justified by faith apart from any works would be impressive to any Jew. The choice is also significant in that Abraham's justification predated his circumcision. He was still a Gentile! Paul will use this fact later in the discussion.

Paul encloses the answer to the question posed in verse 1 concerning Abraham's experience with some potential implications of that experience (Rom. 4:2 and Rom. 4:4-5). If he gained his righteousness through self-effort, he would have reason to boast but this boasting would not be in God but in himself (2 Cor. 10:17). The expression, *not before God* is better translated not toward God. His boast would be directed at himself and not at God. After answering the question, Paul offers a second implication to gaining righteousness by working. God would be indebted to give Abraham eternal life for *the one who works, his wage is not credited as a favor, but as what is due.* On the other hand, if Abraham gained righteousness by faith, his boasting would be in God alone; and his eternal life would be a matter of divine favor. Paul's point is that a system of works leads to self-boasting and excludes the grace of God.

Paul answers the question about Abraham's experience by quoting Gen. 15:6. The story in Genesis 15 and its relationship to the rest of Abraham's life is important. He had already left Ur at God's command (Gen. 12:1-4). Yet, he had no son though God had promised to give him a great family (Gen. 13:14-15). In Gen. 15:4-5, God confirmed His promise that he would have not only a son but descendants as numerous as the stars of the sky. In response, *Abraham believed God and God credited it to him as righteousness.* Though doubts and fears would come, he never lost sight of God's promise.

The term, *credited*, *logidzomai*, found 11 times in the chapter, is an accounting term, meaning to place on one's account either a debit or a credit. The general sense of adding a credit to one's account is found in Rom. 4:4 where it relates work to wages. Here a credit of righteousness is placed on Abraham's account. In 2 Tim. 4:16 the negative idea of adding a charge is found. In Rom. 4:8 a debit or charge is not placed on one's account or is removed; that is, it is forgiven.

4:6-8. Paul offers David as secondary evidence, *Blessed is the man whose sin the lord will not take into account*, quoting from Ps. 32:1-2. Abraham's experience speaks to the gaining of righteousness. David's experience speaks of the removal of unrighteousness, a charge of sin. The term translated *take into account* is the same term, *logidzomai*, translated *credited* in Rom. 4:3, and Rom. 4:6.

Abraham's Justification Not Conditioned on Circumcision
4:9-12

⁹Is this blessing then on the circumcised, or on the uncircumcised also? For we say, "Faith was credited to Abraham as righteousness." ¹⁰How then was it credited? While he was circumcised, or uncircumcised? Not while circumcised, but while uncircumcised;

¹¹and he received the sign of circumcision, a seal of the righteousness of the faith which he had while uncircumcised, so that he might be the father of all who believe without being circumcised, that righteousness might be credited to them, ¹²and the father of circumcision to those who not only are of the circumcision, but who also follow in the steps of the faith of our father Abraham which he had while uncircumcised.

Summary   The blessing of justification by faith is not limited to Jews since Abraham obtained it without being circumcised while a Gentile.

Structural Layout

> Is this blessing upon circumcised or uncircumcised also?
>> How was it reckoned?
>>> while he was uncircumcised.
>>>> Received circumcision
>>>>> a sign
>>>>> a seal of righteousness of faith
>>>> that he might be father of all who believe without circumcision
>>>>> father of circumcision who follow in steps of faith.

4:9-12 Commentary

4:9-10. Now, Paul demonstrates that this blessing of justification by faith came without any condition related to circumcision. That is, circumcision had nothing to do with it; and so, it is not exclusively for the Jews. This is seen by the fact that Abraham had not yet been circumcised when God declared him to be righteous.

The question, *How was it credited?* differs from the question, "When was it reckoned?" The latter would deal only with the timing. Paul's question deals, not with timing, but with method. Righteousness was not credited in conjunction with being circumcised, nor did it involve any works. Thus, uncircumcised Gentiles can receive this blessing. It is not limited to Jews.

4:11-12. Such a conclusion might seem to imply that circumcision had no purpose. This cannot be the case since God instituted circumcision (Gen 17:10). The problem is that Jews incorrectly thought the purpose of circumcision was to establish their righteous standing with God. If circumcision is not purposed to provide righteousness, then what is its purpose? Paul suggests that it is a *sign* and a *seal* of the righteousness that he gained by faith alone. A sign is an outward representation of an inner relationship. In the same way, baptism is a sign of the Christian's salvation. But just like Jewish circumcision, baptism does not result in gaining a righteous standing with God; it merely signifies that one already has it. A seal is an authoritative mark, an identification or guarantee of ownership. For the Christian, the Holy Spirit is our seal (Eph. 4:30). We are not saved because we are sealed. We are sealed because we are saved. So it was with circumcision, God set his seal upon his people, not so that they might become his people but because they were his people.

Thus, Abraham is *the father of all who believe*, whether Jewish (circumcised) or Gentile (uncircumcised). The key is that one's relationship to Abraham is based on faith, not on a ceremonial rite. One must *follow in the steps of the faith of our father Abraham.*

Abraham's Descendants Justified by Faith, Not by Law   *4:13-17*

[13]For the promise to Abraham or to his descendants that he would be heir of the world was not through the Law, but through the righteousness of faith. [14]For if those who are of the Law are heirs, faith is made void and the promise is nullified; [15]for the Law brings about wrath, but where there is no law, there also is no violation. [16]For this reason it is by faith, in order that it may be in accordance with grace, so that the promise will be guaranteed to all the descendants, not only to those who are of the Law, but also to those who are of the faith of Abraham, who is the father of us all, [17](as it is written, "A father of many nations have I made you") in the presence of Him whom he believed, even God, who gives life to the dead and calls into being that which does not exist.

Summary Though the Law was introduced after Abraham, his descendants must also receive the promise by faith, not by Law; otherwise the promise would be nullified.

51

Structural Layout

> The promise to his descendants
>> not through the Law
>> but through the righteousness of faith
> For if those of Law are heirs
>> faith made void
>> promise is nullified
>>> For Law brings wrath
> For this reason it is by faith
>> so that promise will be guaranteed to all descendants
>>> not only those of Law
>>> but also those of faith of Abraham
>>>> Father of us all
>>>>> As it is written
>>>>> "Father of many nations"

4:13-17 Commentary

Next Paul brings the Law into the discussion. The Law, which came 430 years after Abraham (Gal 3:17), might also introduce a change in the way that the descendants gain righteousness. Paul refutes this idea by showing that the original promise was based solely on faith. Changes in methodology, from grace to Law would invalidate the promise. Paul provides a similar argument in Gal. 3:15-22.

4:13. The conjunction, *or* in the expression, *the promise to Abraham or to his descendants*, indicates a shift from speaking about Abraham to speaking about his descendants. At issue is not how Abraham related to this promised justification but how the descendants relate to it. Will these heirs gain the promised in the same way that Abraham did? Paul asserts that, like Abraham, the promised justification must come to the descendants by faith, not through Law.

4:14-15. Paul offers two reasons why it must be the case that the heirs gain the promise by faith. First, if Law is introduced, the promise is *nullified* (Rom. 4:14). This is true because the only condition upon which the promise is based is faith. From Paul's perspective, faith and works of the Law are mutually exclusive. To introduce Law is to *void* faith. If you void faith, then you destroy the promise that is based on it. Second, to introduce Law as a condition immediately leaves the heir in the state of condemnation (Rom. 4:15). *Law* brings *about wrath* (Rom. 3:20). However, when Law is eliminated as a condition, *there is no violation*. This does not mean that the heirs do not sin. Rather, since obedience to Law is not a condition for the promise, God is not obligated to condemn based on violation of the Law.

4:16-17. As a result, the promise is certain to all his *descendants*, both Jews and Gentiles. All who believe are Abraham's descendants since the concept of *father* is related to spiritual heritage, not physical lineage. To be related to one as a spiritual father you must resemble this person in some meaningful way (Luke 8:39). Paul sees *faith* as that resemblance which relates us to Abraham and to the promise given to him. This is in accordance with *grace*. Grace is a manner of acting apart from any condition of merit. For Paul grace and faith are always together. God acts graciously with the only condition being faith (Rom. 5:2, Eph. 2:8). Paul confirms the idea that Abraham is the spiritual father of Gentiles as well as Jews by quoting from Gen 17:5, *A father of many nations have I made you.* He then transitions to a new thought with his closing description of the God in whom Abraham believed. In describing God as the one *who gives life to the dead and calls into being that which does not exist*, Paul alludes to the birth of Isaac (Gen. 17:17, Rom. 4:19), not to the later account of the sacrifice of Isaac.

Abraham's Faith Described   *4:18-22*

[18]In hope against hope he believed, so that he might become a father of many nations according to that which had been spoken, "So shall your descendants be." [19]Without becoming weak in faith he contemplated his own body, now as good as dead since he was about a hundred years old, and the deadness of Sarah's womb; [20]yet, with respect to the promise of God, he did not waver in unbelief but grew strong in faith, giving glory to God, [21]and being fully assured that what God had promised, He was able also to perform. [22]Therefore it was also credited to him as righteousness.

Summary   Because Abraham expressed a dynamic faith in God's promises in spite of outward circumstances, he was declared righteous.

Structural Layout

> In hope against hope
> he believed
>   Without becoming weak in faith
> he contemplated his own body
> he did not waiver in unbelief
> grew strong in faith
>   being fully assured
> Therefore
>   it was reckoned to him

4:18-22 Commentary

In this section, Paul describes the object and quality of Abraham's faith. Paul includes these verses to help define true, saving faith. His claim that justification is by faith requires such a definition. Not every kind of faith is sufficient to justify.

As to the object of his faith, first, he believed in God who could bring life where no life was possible (Rom. 4:17). That this refers to the birth of Isaac is confirmed by the descriptions in this section. Next, he believed in the promise, *So shall your descendants be*, given to him by God (Gen 15:5). Finally, he believed God was *able to perform* His promise.

As to the quality of Abraham's faith, Paul describes it as a dynamic, life-changing faith. It was not static intellectualism. Even though the situation looked hopeless, it *hoped against hope*. He never became *weak in* faith in spite of overwhelming evidence against it. His faith *did not waver* but instead *grew strong*. It was a faith of full assurance.

The *Therefore* at Rom. 4:22 marks the conclusion in which Paul reiterates the quotation from Gen. 15.6. This is the kind of faith that is necessary for God to credit as righteousness. No lesser faith will do. Saving faith is directed at the right object in a dynamic, life-changing way.

Abraham's Experience Validly Applied to Us   *4:23-25*

^{23}*Now not for his sake only was it written that it was credited to him,* ^{24}*but for our sake also, to whom it will be credited, as those who believe in Him who raised Jesus our Lord from the dead,* ^{25}*He who was delivered over because of our transgressions, and was raised because of our justification.*

Summary   The recording of Abraham's experience was purposed to demonstrate that we also are justified by our faith in Jesus who died and was raised for us.

Structural Layout

It was written "It was reckoned to him"
    not for his sake only
    but for our sake also
        to whom it will be reckoned
        who believe in Him
           who raised Jesus
                delivered because of transgression
                raised because of justification

4:23-25 Commentary

Paul now deals with the problem of generalizing the experience of Abraham to the present day. How can we be sure that his experience applies to us? We make an error in logic (hasty generalization) if we generalize the facts without a valid reason to do so.

4:23-24a. Paul argues that the experience of Abraham is validly applied to us since his experience was recorded by God in the Scriptures. *It was written for us.* From this statement, we can gain insight into Paul's understanding of the nature and purpose of Scripture. Scripture does not record history for history's sake. In Scripture, history is salvation-history recorded for our instruction (1 Cor.10:11; 2 Tim.3:16). It is one thing for God to justify Abraham by faith and quite another to record that fact in Scripture. God recorded it for us so that we might understand His ways.

4:24b-25. However, for the experience of Abraham to relate to us, our experience must parallel his experience. Only then can the results validly be applied to us. So, Paul ends the section by showing the parallels between Abraham's experience and our own. Abraham believed in the God who brings to life what is dead (4:17,19). So too, we believe in the God *who raised Jesus Christ from the dead.* He was *delivered up* to death because we were sinners in need of salvation. He *was raised* by the Father because His death secured our justification. The preposition, *because (dia)* should not be translated *for* as is found in several translations. The preposition establishes a causal relationship and is best translated, "because of". The object of the preposition is that which prompts the action modified by the phrase. The need to resolve the problem of sin prompted the Father to deliver up the Son. The sufficiency of that death to produce justification prompted the Father to raise him from the dead. The resurrection confirms the work of Christ on the cross and assures us that we are justified.

Answering the Sufficiency Objection   *5:1-21*

Summary   Justification by faith is certain in spite of present tribulation and is sufficient to overcome condemnation

Structural Layout

      having been justified by faith,
we also exult in our tribulations,
      Much more
we shall be from the wrath of God

      by the transgression of the one,
death reigned through the one,
      much more
those will reign in life through the One, Jesus Christ.
      who receive the gift of righteousness

Overview

The section is designed as a rebuttal to two objections to Paul's thesis. The first objection deals with present sufferings (Rom. 5:1-11). How can Paul claim to be right with God when He is experiencing such tribulation in this world? Doesn't this suffering refute his claim that he has a righteous standing with God? The second section deals with the objection that Christ's death is a sufficient remedy for the sinfulness of all men (Rom. 5:12-21). How can the actions of one man secure righteousness for all men?

Why these two objections are introduced together is difficult to understand. However, several literary features found in both units suggest that the two should be considered together. First, both units shift from the past experience in sin (Rom. 5:6-8, Rom. 5:12-14), to the present experience of justification (Rom. 5:1, 5:16, 18), and then to the future experience of final salvation (Rom. 5:9-10, Rom. 5:17, 19). Second, the use of *much more* in both units (Rom. 5:9, Rom. 5:10, Rom. 5:15, Rom. 5:17, and Rom. 5:20) suggests that Paul is demonstrating that this justification is more than sufficient to assure our future salvation. In spite of these objections, we can be certain about our future and about the sufficiency of our justification.

Most classical commentaries place Romans 5 with Rom. 3:21-4:25. Several modern scholars see Romans 5 being more closely associated with Romans 6-8. Though this has merit, it seems that Romans 6-8 forms too tight an argument to include the material found in Romans 5. It is more likely that Romans 5 stands alone as a short answer to objections concerning the certainty and sufficiency of justification by faith in Jesus Christ to bring about future salvation.

Certainty of Future Salvation in Spite of Tribulation   5:1-11

[1]Therefore, having been justified by faith, we have peace with God through our Lord Jesus Christ, [2]through whom also we have obtained our introduction by faith into this grace in which we stand; and we exult in hope of the glory of God.

[3]And not only this, but we also exult in our tribulations, knowing that tribulation brings about perseverance; [4]and perseverance, proven character; and proven character, hope;

[5]and hope does not disappoint, because the love of God has been poured out within our hearts through the Holy Spirit who was given to us. [6]For while we were still helpless,

at the right time Christ died for the ungodly. ⁷For one will hardly die for a righteous man; though perhaps for the good man someone would dare even to die. ⁸But God demonstrates His own love toward us, in that while we were yet sinners, Christ died for us. ⁹Much more then, having now been justified by His blood, we shall be saved from the wrath of God through Him. ¹⁰For if while we were enemies we were reconciled to God through the death of His Son, much more, having been reconciled, we shall be saved by His life.

¹¹And not only this, but we also exult in God through our Lord Jesus Christ, through whom we have now received the reconciliation.

Summary   In spite of present tribulation, we do have peace with God and are assured of future salvation because of God's love.

Structural Layout

> having been justified by faith,
> we have peace with God
> we also exult in our tribulations,
> knowing hope does not disappoint,
> because the love of God has been poured out
> ⁶For
> while helpless,
> Christ died for ungodly.
> while we were yet sinners,
> Christ died for us.
> ⁹Much more then,
> we shall be saved from wrath
> ¹⁰For
> if while we were enemies
> we were reconciled to God
> through the death of His Son,
> much more,
> having been reconciled,
> we shall be saved by His life.
> we also exult in God
> through our Lord Jesus Christ,
> through whom we have now received the reconciliation.

5:1-11 Commentary

Many commentators understand this section to be a description of the fruits or results of justification. However, if this were the case, we would expect a simple sequential organization of the material. Instead, we see a very complex argument. The passage is organized around the three-fold statement, *we* exult (Rom. 5:1, 3, 11). This is made even clearer by the repetition of *not only this but … also* preceding the second and third iterations. When the passage is divided based on this marking (Rom. 5:1-2, Rom. 5:3-10, Rom. 5:11), it become clear that the major development is found in 5:3-11. This section deals with tribulations (Rom. 5:3). Thus, 5:1-11 is designed to answer the objection to justification by faith that present tribulation demonstrates that Paul and those that follow his gospel are not justified. If it is true that they justified and therefore has peace with God, why are they under such tribulation? Doesn't this tribulation indicate that God is still angry with them? Paul also handles this objection in Rom. 8:18-39. The two sections share important lexical concepts: suffering (Rom. 5:3, Rom. 8:18); hope (Rom. 5:1-2, Rom. 8:20-25); glory (Rom. 5:2, Rom. 8:18-21); and love (Rom. 5:5-8, Rom. 8:35-39).

5:1-2. Paul begins by strongly affirming his total confidence in his justification. The result of being justified is *peace with God*. Peace with God means that God is no longer angry with us. This is in contrast to the wrath of God mentioned in Rom. 1:18 and Rom. 2:5. We are now friends with God through Jesus Christ. Through him *we have obtained our introduction into this grace*. Jesus provided a way into God's favor. As a result, *we exult in hope of the glory of God*. Paul is describing our future glory in heaven. Hope is always directed toward the future. Paul has in mind standing in heaven and being surrounded with God's glory. When this occurs, we will ourselves be glorified (Rom. 8:18-21). So, Paul with highly emotive language expresses his full confidence that the Christian's current justification will indeed result in glorification, our final salvation. It is this conclusion that is made in Rom. 5:9-10.

5:3-4. Next, Paul introduces the objection to this hope, namely that present *tribulations* disprove his hope. Paul deals with the same objection in Rom. 8:18-25. However, there he used the word *sufferings* (*pathēma*). Here, Paul uses *tribulation* (*thlipsis*) because of its negative connotation that would be more in keeping with the interlocutor's objection. Though tribulation can have a neutral sense of affliction without reference to the cause, Paul selects the word because of its association with God's wrath (Rom. 2:9, Deut. 31:17; Zeph. 1:15 LXX), giving it a very negative connotation of divine judgment. The Lord also used it in this sense in his Olivet Discourse (Matt 24:21). The occurrence of wrath in the immediate context confirms this intent (Rom. 5:9). So, the objection is: You are not justified or have peace with God since he continues to pour out his wrath upon you.

Paul rejects the objection first by *exulting* in this tribulation and then by demonstrating that tribulation rather than destroying our hope actually leads us to greater hope. *Tribulation brings about perseverance.* Paul rejects the negative connotation in his sufferings and instead sees that sufferings are positive tools that God uses in our lives. Perseverance (*hupomonē*) is the ability to remain under extreme pressure or weight. *Hupomonē* can have the idea of endurance. This results in *proven character, dokimē* or proof that validates. When we endure the trials of life, we prove that God's grace is working in us. Such proof leads to *hope,* our assurance and confidence that we are God's and that a glorious future awaits us. Thus, we go full circle and arrive right back to the hope in which we exult (Rom 5:2). So, tribulation does not destroy our hope, it produces it.

5:5-10. Paul next explains why he can be so sure. Might *this hope disappoint* you? Paul is not referring to any hope, but specifically to the hope that he has proclaimed in Rom. 5:2-4. The Greek article found with hope in Rom. 5:5 is an article of previous reference and can validly be translated *this hope about which I am speaking.* This assurance of future glory will not *disappoint* us. It will not result in our dishonor or disgrace. Paul demonstrates this by arguing from the lesser to the greater situation concerning the *love of God.* The argument is introduced in 5:6 with the word, *For (gar). gar* introduces support or an explanation for a statement just given. In this instance, it introduces the reason why this hope will not disappoint. In the past when we were *helpless, ungodly, sinners,* and *enemies,* God loved us by sending Christ to die for us, providing righteousness and peace. Now, in the present, we have a superior position with God. We are *justified* (Rom. 5:9) and *reconciled* (Rom.

5:10). The result of justification is righteousness and the result of reconciliation is peace (Eph. 2:14-16, Col. 1:20). So, we can be *much more* assured that our future is secure, *we shall be saved from wrath.* The sections began with the assertion that we have peace with God and ends with the assertion that this peace (reconciliation) insures our future salvation. Christ's death secured this salvation and *his life* assures it.

5:11. Paul closes the section with a final word of exultation. As he considers this truth, he is compelled not only to exult in the hope of God, not only in his tribulation, but to *exult in God* himself. God Himself, the very one who has loved us and secured our peace is the one who should fill our hearts with adoration and praise (Ps. 31:11 LXX).

Sufficiency of Christ's Death to Provide Justification 5:12-21

[12]Therefore, just as through one man sin entered into the world, and death through sin, and so death spread to all men, because all sinned— [13]for until the Law sin was in the world, but sin is not imputed when there is no law. [14]Nevertheless death reigned from Adam until Moses, even over those who had not sinned in the likeness of the offense of Adam, who is a type of Him who was to come.

[15]But the free gift is not like the transgression. For if by the transgression of the one the many died, much more did the grace of God and the gift by the grace of the one Man, Jesus Christ, abound to the many. [16]The gift is not like that which came through the one who sinned; for on the one hand the judgment arose from one transgression resulting in condemnation, but on the other hand the free gift arose from many transgressions resulting in justification. [17]For if by the transgression of the one, death reigned through the one, much more those who receive the abundance of grace and of the gift of righteousness will reign in life through the One, Jesus Christ.

[18]So then as through one transgression there resulted condemnation to all men, even so through one act of righteousness there resulted justification of life to all men. [19]For as through the one man's disobedience the many were made sinners, even so through the obedience of the One the many will be made righteous.

[20]The Law came in so that the transgression would increase; but where sin increased, grace abounded all the more, [21]so that, as sin reigned in death, even so grace would reign through righteousness to eternal life through Jesus Christ our Lord.

Summary Just as condemnation came by the one man, Adam, so also justification comes in abundance by the one man, Jesus Christ.

Structural Layout

just as
                through one man—Adam, who is a type of Him who was to come
        sin entered into the world
        death through sin
death spread to all men,
        because all sinned
death reigned from Adam until Moses

much more
                of the one Man, Jesus Christ
        did the grace abound to the many
        the free gift *arose* from many transgressions resulting in justification
        those who receive the abundance of grace will reign in life

So then
                as through one transgression
        there resulted condemnation to all men,
                even so through one act of righteousness
        there resulted justification of life to all men.
                as through the one man's disobedience
        the many were made sinners,
                even so through the obedience of the One
        the many will be made righteous.

The Law came in
        so that the transgression would increase
   but
        where sin increased,
grace abounded all the more
        so that,
                as sin reigned in death,
                even so grace would reign through Jesus Christ our Lord.

5:12-21 Commentary

In this section, Paul answers the objection that one man cannot secure righteousness for all men. How can one man's death pay the price for all men's sin? Paul argues that since one man, Adam, brought about the condemnation of all men through his one act of sin, Christ can also bring about the justification of all men through his one act of obedience. The adjective, *one* (*one man, one transgression; one act of righteousness; one man's disobedience; and the obedience of the one*) dominates the section (Rom. 5:12, Rom. 5:15-18). Though some see the section merely as a comparison between Christ and Adam because of Paul's use of *just as* and *so also*, the additional logical connectors, *for* (*gar*), *so then* (*ara oun*), *so that* (*hina*) suggest that it is more than a simple comparison; it is an argument -- an argument from analogy. Paul employs if...then logic (Rom. 5:15, Rom. 5:17), and he provides a conclusion to the argument with *so then* (Rom. 5:18).

The assumption in the argument is that universal sin, death, and condemnation are the results of one man's disobedience. This theological assumption is appropriate for a Jewish interlocutor. It is based on the story of sin's entrance into the world in Gen 3:1-19 and is a common assumption used by Paul (1 Cor.15:22; 1 Cor.15:45; 1 Tim.2:13-14). Modern Christian apologists are for the sufficiency of Christ's payment on the basis of his deity. This, however, would not be a logical starting point for Paul, since the Jews did not accept the deity of Christ. So, instead, Paul argues from the imputation of sin in Adam, a position that most Jews in Paul's day would affirm.

The section contains four parts. First, Paul supports the assumption that sin and death entered the world through Adam's sin (Rom. 5:12-14). Next, Paul argues that Christ's act of righteousness is more than sufficient to overcome the universal sin and death brought about by Adam (Rom. 5:15-17). He then draws the conclusion that Christ's act of obedience results in justification (Rom. 5:18-19). Finally, he explains the place of the Law in this scheme (Rom. 5:20-21).

5:12-14. Paul begins by stating that the current state of universal sin and death is the result of Adam's sin. The *just as through one man* introduces the first part of the comparison between Adam and Christ but the second part which would be introduced by *so also* is missing though it is clearly understood based on its presence later in the argument (Rom. 5:18-19). This entrance of sin through Adam resulted in the total dominance of *sin* and *death* in the lives of all people (Rom. 7:21-23, Rom. 5:14).

So, death spread to all men because all sinned. In what sense did all sin? Augustine suggested that we participated in Adam's sin. When Adam sinned, we sinned. Like Levi who paid tithes to Melchizedek while in the body of his father (Heb. 7:9-10), we sinned while in the body of Adam. Others suggest that Adam was the representative or federal head for the race. God knew that the whole race would do what Adam did. Still others explain that Adam's sin left a defect upon the race so profound that as a result every person sins. In this view, the sin nature passed down from parent to child results in every person sinning. Though these theories can be debated, what cannot be debates is the final result. *Death spread to all men, because all sinned.* One man was the cause of universal sin and death.

Rom. 5:13-14 are understood differently depending on whether you see *all sinned* to refer to imputed sin in Adam or to personal sin in time. Those who understand *all sinned* as imputed sin in Adam understand the verses as proving that sin is imputed in Adam. Personal acts of sin were in the world from the time of Adam even though the Law had not yet been given. Yet, God did not count these acts of sin against people (*sin is not imputed*) because Torah Law had not yet been given. Nevertheless, all people died as a result of sin. So, the sin that resulted in their death could not have been their personal acts sin. It was the sin imputed of Adam. This interpretation has several weaknesses. First, it seems clear from Genesis that prior to the Law God did hold people responsible for their personal acts of sin (Gen 6:5). Second, it requires that *sin* be understood in two very different ways in the same context, personal sin and imputed sin. This is unlikely.

Those who understand *all sinned* as personal acts of sin understand the verses as proving the universality of sin. Prior to the Law all people sinned yet they were not as aware of their own sinfulness. This is the understanding of the statement *sin is not imputed.* The verb, *ellogeō* is similar to *logizomai* translated *credited* throughout Rom. 4. In Rom. 4, God was the one crediting an account with righteousness or sinfulness. The prior interpretation retains this idea.

However, since the verb is passive and no agent for the action is supplied, it can refer to the act of the individual who fails to credit sin to his or her own account. That is, this individual fails to recognize that sin is an offense against God. Two ideas support this conclusion. First, this is the way *logizomai* is used in Rom. 6:11. In that context, Paul encourages us to place on our own account our death to sin, the very thing that God has already place on our account (Rom. 6:1-6). Second, Paul indicates that Law brings about recognition of sin (Rom. 3:20, Rom. 7:7). So, even though individuals were less aware of the sinfulness of their acts, the fact that they died made it clear that God held it against them even though they did not sin like Adam. That is, they did not violate an external law. Instead, they violated conscience (Rom. 2:14-16).

5:15-17. Having established the fact that Adam's sin resulted in universal sin and death, Paul now argues for the sufficiency of Christ's one act of obedience to overcome the results of the one act of disobedience. The use of *much more*, *abounds*, and *abundance* makes Paul's point clear. Christ's act of obedience, His death on the cross (Phil. 2:8), is more than sufficient to overcome the results of Adam's sin. Sin, condemnation, and death are replaced with righteousness, justification, and life. He begins by comparing the *free gift* with Adam's transgression. What is this free gift? It cannot be justification or righteousness since in Rom. 5:16 the free gift results in justification. The gift is Christ's redeeming work, which is the basis for this justification (Rom. 3:24-25). The term for gift, *charisma*, emphasizes that this gift is the result of divine grace (*charis*) and it is synonymous to the expression, *a gift by His grace* found in Rom. 3:24.

The use of *for if* in Rom. 5:15 and Rom. 5:17 suggests that Paul is doing more than comparing Christ and Adam; he is arguing for the sufficiency of Christ's work. This conditional argument would go something like this, "If one man's disobedience resulted in the death of many, then one man's obedience will result in life for many." Yet, this argument is only valid if the two men are at least equal in comparison. Paul seems to be arguing with the supposition that Jesus is greater than Adam. Adam is merely a *type of the one who is to come* (Rom.

5:14). In Scripture, a type is an Old Testament prophetic prefiguring of some New Testament person or event. The New Testament fulfillment is superior to the Old Testament type (Heb. 8:5-6). Jesus is no mere man; he is the *Christ.* As such, his work can result in *much more* than the work of Adam. Adam's act was the result of human motivation; Christ's act was the result of *the grace of God.* In grace, God acts to do what otherwise cannot be done (Rom. 8:3). This grace is given in *abundance.* Thus, the reign of death brought on by condemnation is replaced by *the reign in life.* Yet, this grace is channeled only *through the One, Jesus Christ.* It is only efficacious to *those who receive* the gift he has secured for them.

5:18-19. *So then* introduces Paul's conclusion that is expressed in two parallel sentences. In the first sentence condemnation is replaced with justification. In the second sentence, sin is replaced with righteousness. The two sentences are not synonymous but logically connected. The second sentence states the alternative conditions and the first sentence the alternate consequences. Since righteousness replaces sinfulness, it must also be true that justification replaces condemnation.

How are we to understand Paul's statement, *there resulted justification of life to all men?* It cannot be the case that Paul is affirming that eventually all will be justified—a form of universalism. First, Paul has already limited those who receive this justification to *those who receive the abundance of grace and of the gift of righteousness* (Rom. 5:17). Second, it is clear from his condemnation of both Jews and Gentiles that Paul did not accept universal justification (Rom. 1:18-3:20). Either we must limit the meaning of *justification* or limit the meaning of *all.* Those who limit the meaning of justification suggest that Christ's work has made justification for all men possible. From God's perspective, all can be justified; but from man's perspective only those who accept the gift will actually be justified. The disadvantage of this view is that it requires justification to be understood differently than it is in the rest of the passage. Those who limit the meaning of all suggest that all is limited to all who are related to Christ. All those who are related to Adam (every person) have been affected by Adam's sin; all those who are related to Christ (believers) are affected by Christ's obedience. The disadvantage of this view is that it weakens the universal scope of Paul's argument.

5:20-21. Paul ends the section by explaining the place of Torah Law in this scheme. The Jews saw the Law as a means of escape (Rom. 2:3) from the sinful condition brought about by Adam. From Paul's perspective, rather than making things better, the introduction of Law made things worse. One of God's purposes in giving the Law was *that transgression would increase.* In what sense does transgression increase? Two ideas seem to be present. First, sin existed before the Law; but with the coming of Law sin became transgression—a willful disobedience to a known rule (Rom. 5:20). This, however, does not seem to be all that Paul meant since in Rom. 5:21 he says that *sin increased* not just transgression. Law actually resulted in more acts of sin since in some sense sinful passions are aroused by the Law (Rom. 7:5). Yet, in spite of the increase in sin, *grace abounded all the more.* No amount of sin can exhaust the grace of God. The result is that *grace reigns through righteousness to eternal life through Jesus Christ our Lord.* Clearly, Christ's work of grace is sufficient to overcome all sin.

Answering the Antinomian Objection   6:1-8:39

Summary   Justification by faith does not promote a life of sin but rather through the Spirit provides the victory over sin that Law can never provide.

Structural Layout

> Are we to continue is sin?   Never!
>> We died to sin.
>> no longer slaves to sin
>> Walk in newness of life
>> Wages of sin is death → gift of God eternal life

> You were made to die to the Law
>> while in flesh,
>> sinful passions aroused by Law bear fruit for death
>> now, released from Law...
>> serve in newness of Spirit

> Is the Law sin?
>> May it never be!
>> Sin deceived me, killed me
>> I joyfully concur with Law
>> the Law is holy
>> I am sold into bondage to sin
>> wretched man that I am!

> Law of Spirit has set you free
>> requirement of Law met in us who walk according to Spirit
>> you are not in flesh but in Spirit
>> Spirit is life, will give life to mortal bodies
>> under obligation, not to the flesh

Overview

In this section, Paul answers another objection to justification by faith. Won't this process, in which God by grace just forgives sin and credits as righteous those that are not, encourage people to sin even more? This antinomian objection is based on the thought that law is necessary to produce proper behavior. Take away the consequences of violating law (Rom. 5:20) and you open the door to moral anarchy.

Paul argues that it is only in life under grace in the Spirit that we can find victory over sin and the ability to live for God (Rom. 6:14, Rom. 7:6, Rom. 8:2). In our union with Christ we have died to sin, gaining release from its enslavement and have been raised with Him, gaining the ability to live for God (Rom. 6:1-23).

The alternative, life under Law in the flesh (Rom. 7:1-25), is incapable of producing holiness and results in death (Rom. 7:5). Yet, the problem is not with the Law (Rom. 7:12, Rom. 7:14), but with sin-enslaved humanity (Rom. 7:8, Rom. 7:13, Rom. 7:17, Rom. 7:20). In this wretched state, people are frustrated; wanting to do what they acknowledge is right but totally incapable of doing so (Rom. 7:7:21-24). They live under the principle of sin and death.

In contrast, the Christian lives under the Spirit's principle of life (Rom. 8:1-39). By the Spirit we are set free from the principle of sin and death and are now able to live for God. The Christian is no longer obligated to the old life but now has freedom in the family of God to live for Him. No amount of suffering negates the fact that we are spiritually alive.

Thus, Paul demonstrates that the legalistic approach to holy living promoted by the Judaizers is doomed to failure because it relies on impotent humanity; and that the grace approach to holy living connected with justification by faith will succeed because it relies on the power of God.

Union with Christ Provides Release from Sin   6:1-23

Summary   Justification by faith does not promote a life of sin but provides release from sin's deadly enslavement through our union with Christ.

Structural Layout

> Are we to continue is sin?   Never!
> We died to sin.
> > no longer slaves to sin
> > sin shall not be master over you
>
> Walk in newness of life
> > likeness of His resurrection
> > alive to God
>
> Shall we sin not under Law?   Never!
> you are a slave to whom you obey
> > sin leading to death
> > obedience leading to life

Overview

In chapter six, Paul begins to answer the antinomian objection to justification by faith, namely that the removal of law under grace will encourage people to sin even more (Rom. 6:1, Rom. 6:15). He suggests that our union with Christ is in direct contrast to a life of sin. In this section, our union with Christ becomes the key to our sanctification. Salvation has brought about a transformation in the spiritual dynamic of our lives. We died and rose with Christ and now we can live for God.

The paralleled rhetorical questions in Rom. 6:1 and Rom. 6:15 mark off the two sections. In the first section, Paul argues that our union in Christ provides release from sin's enslavement. (Rom. 6:1-14). We died and rose with Christ and therefore we are dead to sin (Rom. 6:2), released from sin's power (Rom. 6:7), and now able to live a victorious life for God (Rom. 6:4, Rom. 6:11, Rom. 6:13).

In the second section, Paul reminds us that following sin leads to death (Rom. 6:15-23). It is absurd for the Christian who has escaped the deadly results of sin to return to it (Rom. 6:16, Rom. 6:21, Rom. 6:23). We are now the slaves of God (Rom. 6:18, Rom. 6:22) resulting in life (Rom. 6:22-23). We must follow Him in sanctification.

Freedom from Sin's Dominion Through Our Union with Christ
6:1-14

[1]What shall we say then? Are we to continue in sin so that grace may increase? [2]May it never be! How shall we who died to sin still live in it? [3]Or do you not know that all of us who have been baptized into Christ Jesus have been baptized into His death? [4]Therefore we have been buried with Him through baptism into death, so that as Christ was raised from the dead through the glory of the Father, so we too might walk in newness of life. [5]For if we have become united with Him in the likeness of His death, certainly we shall also be in the likeness of His resurrection, [6]knowing this, that our old self was crucified with Him, in order that our body of sin might be done away with, so that we would no longer be slaves to sin; [7]for he who has died is freed from sin. [8]Now if we have died with Christ, we believe that we shall also live with Him, [9]knowing that Christ, having been raised from the dead, is never to die again; death no longer is master over Him. [10]For the death that He died, He died to sin once for all; but the life that He lives, He lives to God. [11]Even so consider yourselves to be dead to sin, but alive to God in Christ Jesus.

[12]Therefore do not let sin reign in your mortal body so that you obey its lusts, [13]and do not go on presenting the members of your body to sin as instruments of unrighteousness; but present yourselves to God as those alive from the dead, and your members as instruments of righteousness to God. [14]For sin shall not be master over you, for you are not under law but under grace.

Summary   It is absurd for the Christian who has died to sin's domination to continue to live in it.

Structural Layout

> Are we to continue is sin?   Never!
> > We died to sin.
> > baptized into Christ's death
> > > that we might walk in newness of life.
> > > if united in likeness of His death
> > we shall be in likeness of His resurrection
> > our old self crucified
> > > that we no longer be slaves of sin.
> Therefore
> > do not let sin reign
> > do not go on presenting to sin... but present... to God... alive
> > > For sin shall not have dominion over you

6:1-14 Commentary

Paul begins by introduction the antinomian objection and rejecting it (Rom. 6:1-2a). Paul answers the objection by showing that our union with Christ provides release from sin's enslavement (Rom. 6:2-11). The section progresses from what we should know (Rom. 6:3, Rom. 6:6, Rom. 6:9) about the implications of our union with Christ (Rom. 6:1-11) to how we should respond (Rom. 6:12-13). Paul closes with a final word of assurance concerning our release of sin's enslavement (6:14).

6:1-2a. Following the diatribe style, Paul uses a rhetorical question to introduce an objection from the Jewish interlocutor. *Are we to continue in sin so that grace may increase?* The objection is derived from Paul's statement about grace in Rom. 5:20 that *where sin increased, grace abounded all the more.* It suggests that such unmerited favor, which forgives sin without consequence, will most certainly lead to more sin. Since God would not condone a system that leads to such moral anarchy, Paul's concept of grace must be wrong. This is exactly what Paul's opposition charged Paul with in Rom. 3:8. Paul rejects this conclusion in his diatribe style with the words *may it never be!*

6:2b. Paul begins his response to the objection with another rhetorical question. *How shall we who died to sin still live it?* For Paul, the fact that by grace those who are justified have died to sin is the reason why grace does not lead to moral anarchy. In what sense have Christians died to sin? Some understand it as simply the duty to follow Christ's example; others the act of renouncing sin through repentance; or the fact that we are no longer under condemnation for sin; or even sinless perfection. The context supports the idea that our union with Christ's death has broken sin's power to enslave us (Rom. 6:6-7, Rom. 6:14). This is the sense in which we have died to sin. We have died to sin's enslavement (Rom. 6:18).

6:3-4. This union with Christ is described as being *baptized into Christ Jesus* (Rom. 6:3). Though many claim it to be, this is not water baptism, but Spirit baptism (1 Cor. 12:13). This is supported by several facts. First, we were baptized *into Christ*, not into water (Rom. 6:3). Second, our spiritual union with Christ is in view (Rom. 6:5). This baptism unites us with Christ's death and resurrection. This union could only occur in conjunction with our justification at the point of salvation, not at a later time. Finally, it is clear throughout Romans that Paul sees faith alone as the key to our relationship with God and thus to our union with Christ. Even those who see water baptism in this passage emphasize that it must thus be taken symbolically or metaphorically. Water baptism is a picture and outward symbol of Spirit baptism. However, the two must not be confused.

In Rom. 6:4 Paul expands upon this union with Christ. Our union with Christ not only unites with his death, it also unites us with his resurrection (Rom. 6:5) and results in our ability to *walk in newness of life*. This new life is the regenerated life of the Christian and implies a new ability to live in conformity to God's will (Rom. 6:10-11, Rom. 6:13).

6:5-10. That being raised with Christ is part of our union with Christ is demonstrated through the use of two parallel conditional sentences in Rom. 6:5 and Rom. 6:8. The future tenses in the apodoses of these sentences do not refer to the future resurrection of the body, but are futures of logical result and refer to our current spiritual resurrection. This is supported by several observations. First, the explanations that follow the conditional statements (Rom. 6:6-7 and Rom. 6:9-10) develop the idea of victory over sin in the present life of the believer. Second, these verses expand upon the idea of present resurrection life introduced in Rom. 6:4. Finally, the purpose of the section is not to give hope about a future bodily resurrection, but to encourage believers to appropriate this resurrection life in their current lives (Rom. 6:11, Rom. 6:13).

Each of the conditional sentences is expanded, the first in Rom. 6:6-7 and the second in Rom. 6:9-10. The first explanation in Rom. 6:6-7 focuses on the effects our union with Christ's death has on us with its implications to our current life. In our union with Christ *our old self was crucified with Him.* The old self refers to our old life in Adam, a life of enslavement to sin. With our union with Christ this old life was crucified. Paul is not speaking about an old depraved nature that continues on with the Christian, for this old self was crucified, not merely diminished. It is dead. What has died is our enslavement to sin. The result is that *our body of sin might be done away with*. The most likely understanding of body of sin is that Paul is referring to our bodies as being infected with and dominated by sin. Our union with Christ takes away this domination or renders it powerless. As a result, *we should no longer be slaves to sin*. We are *freed from sin*. The implication is that we can now live for God.

The second explanation in Rom. 6:9-10 focuses on the effects of Christ's resurrection upon himself with clear implications for us. Christ's resurrection involved a full and complete victory over death. *Death no longer is master over Him.* This is true because *He died to sin once for all.* Paul uses the same terminology to refer to Christ's death to sin as he does with that of the believer (Rom. 6:2). Though Christ was not enslaved to sin in the same way that fallen humanity is enslaved to sin, He did live in this sinful world in the likeness of sinful flesh (Rom. 8:3) and did, by taking on our penalty, become sin for us (2 Cor.5:21). This all ended with His death. Now, raised from the dead, *He lives for God.* The implication is not that He was not living for God in the past, but that He now exclusively lives for God with no need to deal with sin. His work of dying for sin has ended.

6:11. The implication of these facts about Christ (Rom. 6:9-10) is given in Rom. 6:11. Since we are united with Christ in His death and resurrection, we should *consider* ourselves *to be dead to sin* and *alive to God. Consider* (*logizomai*) is the same verb used by Paul in chapter four where God *credited* righteousness to Abraham. God placed righteousness on Abraham's account. Now Paul encourages us to place on our account the truth that we have died to sin and are alive to God. This relates to our attitude toward sin and victory over it. We should not live with a defeatist attitude but with a victorious attitude. Rather than being shocked by a few victories over sin, we should be shocked by any defeats.

6:12-13. Paul applies these truths directly with several commands. First, we must not *let sin reign in our mortal bodies*. Our union with Christ has released us from sin's enslavement but this release does not guarantee that we will live in this freedom. It is possible for the Christian to voluntarily re-enslave himself to sin (Rom. 6:16). Now that we have the power to do so, we must remove sin from the throne of our lives. This will result in *not presenting the members of our body to sin*. The idea from the context is that of presenting yourself as a slave to another for service (Rom. 6:16-17). Both negative exhortations are in the Greek present tense and may have the thrust of stopping an activity in which you are already involved. We are to stop letting sin reign and to stop presenting the members of our body to sin. The opposite is to *present yourselves to God*. In this instance, the verb is in the Greek aorist tense. The imperative verb in the aorist tense is found in Rom. 12:1 where it seems to have the sense of presenting completely from start to finish. Such a presentation is possible because we are *alive from the dead* in our union with Jesus Christ.

6:14. Paul concludes the exhortations with a final word of promise that confirms the fact that we can perform what is encouraged. *For sin shall not be master over you.* The future tense is gnomic and represents what will always be true. This must be the case for several reasons. First, the statement summarizes the main theological consequence to our union with Christ (Rom. 6:6-7). Second, this freedom from sin's mastery is reiterated in the next section also (Rom. 6:16-17, Rom. 6:22). Finally, this freedom from sin is because we are *not under Law but under grace*. Paul speaks about Law and grace as systems. As a system Law requires human effort to meet God's righteous standards (Rom. 8:3). As a system grace provides divine assistance to meet God's righteous standards. Our union with Christ is part of the system of grace. Law provides no remedy for our enslavement to sin; but grace does. It is important to distinguish between Law as a system and Law as a moral standard. Both Law and grace reflect the same moral standard. The moral laws of the Law are reflected in the system of grace. Indeed, all of the moral standards of Law are reiterated in the new system of grace. So, to be released from Law does not mean that those under grace are free from moral standards. What is different is not the moral standards but the means by which these standards can be attained.

Freed from Slavery to Sin unto Slavery to God   *6:15-23*

[15]*What then? Shall we sin because we are not under law but under grace? May it never be!*

[16]*Do you not know that when you present yourselves to someone as slaves for obedience, you are slaves of the one whom you obey, either of sin resulting in death, or of obedience resulting in righteousness?* [17]*But thanks be to God that though you were slaves of sin, you became obedient from the heart to that form of teaching to which you were committed,* [18]*and having been freed from sin, you became slaves of righteousness.*

[19]*I am speaking in human terms because of the weakness of your flesh. For just as you presented your members as slaves to impurity and to lawlessness, resulting in further lawlessness, so now present your members as slaves to righteousness, resulting in sanctification.* [20]*For when you were slaves of sin, you were free in regard to righteousness.* [21]*Therefore what benefit were you then deriving from the things of which you are now ashamed? For the outcome of those things is death.* [22]*But now having been freed from sin and enslaved to God, you derive your benefit, resulting in sanctification, and the outcome, eternal life.* [23]*For the wages of sin is death, but the free gift of God is eternal life in Christ Jesus our Lord.*

Summary   The Christian, who has been freed from slavery to sin leading to eternal death and who is now the slave of God leading to eternal life, must live in obedience and righteousness.

Structural Layout

Shall we sin because we are not under law but under grace?
May it never be!
    when you present yourselves *as* slaves
you are slaves of the one whom you obey,
        of sin resulting in death,
        of obedience resulting in righteousness?
    Though you were slaves of sin,
you became obedient
    having been freed from sin,
you became slaves of righteousness.

just as you presented your members as slaves to impurity
so now present your members as slaves to righteousness
    For
        when you were slaves of sin,

you were free in regard to righteousness.
the outcome of those things is death.
now having been freed from sin and enslaved to God,
you derive your benefit, resulting in sanctification
the outcome, eternal life.
For
the wages of sin is death,
the free gift of God is eternal life in Christ Jesus our Lord.

6:15-23 Commentary

Paul provides a second reason for not continuing in sin. Sin is deadly (Rom. 6:16, 21, 23). If you choose to be the slave of sin, you will die. However, choosing to be the slave of God results in righteousness, sanctification, and life.

6:15. This section repeats the objection posed in Rom. 6:1 but does so for a slightly differ reason. The objection arises out of Paul's statement that we are not under Law but under grace (Rom. 6:14). The objection is based on a misunderstanding of the phrase *under Law*. The Jewish interlocutor views Law as God's divine standard and understands Paul's system of grace as a system that undermines this divine standard. With such an assumption, it would be logical to conclusion that the elimination of Law would motivate people to even greater sin. Paul rejects this conclusion using the standard rejection formula of his diatribe style, *May it never be!* He answers the objection in Rom. 6:16-23.

6:16. Paul begins with a principle *when you present yourself to someone for obedience, you are slaves of the one you obey.* By this Paul indicates that everyone is by choice someone's slave. The verb, *present*, ties the section back to Rom. 6:13. Paul uses the present tense to indicate habitual action. When you habitually obey someone, you are that person's slave.

Paul sees only two possible masters: *sin resulting in death or obedience resulting in righteousness.* The person who habitually follows sin and is the slave of sin will come to *death.* Paul is not suggesting that believers will lose eternal life but is suggesting that those individuals who continue in a lifestyle of sin remain under sin and will only gain eternal death. Yet at the same time Paul is warning his Christian readers that sin is a deadly force. Sin in the life of a Christian can lead to physical death, kills fellowship with God, destroys relationships, and murders our testimony. Through the section Paul continues to emphasize the deadly results of following sin (Rom. 6:21, Rom. 6:23).

In contrast, the person who chooses to be the obedient slave of God will come to *righteousness*. This choice is the choice of faith for true obedience is the product of faith (Rom. 1:5). The contrast between death and righteousness does not seem parallel. We would have expected Paul to contrast life with death as he does in Rom. 6:21-22 and in Rom. 6:23. His contrast is purposeful. He does so to introduce the concept of being a slave to righteousness that he develops in the following verses (Rom. 6:17-20). Since righteousness is what is required to gain eternal life (Matt 25:46), it is an appropriate parallel to death by means of metonymy.

6:17-18. Having established the fact that slavery to sin will result in eternal death and that slavery to obedience will result in righteousness and eternal life, Paul next expresses his confidence that the readers have indeed chosen to enslave themselves to obedience and righteousness. Before their salvation they *were the slaves of sin* but when they were saved they *became obedient from the heart*. Paul is not implying that they became sinless but that they had in faith renounced sin and had chosen instead to make obedience to God the goal of their lives. *That form of teaching to which you were committed* is the object of their obedience. Form, *typos*, here takes on the idea of pattern or model. The gospel has within it a pattern or model of righteousness. Its ethical standard is even more rigorous than that of the Law, for it requires that this standard be internalized. It was correctly identified as a way (Acts 9:2). Verse 18 repeats the thought in a more condensed way. They were *freed from sin* and *became slaves of righteousness*. Enslavement to sin is a thing of the past. With our acceptance of Christ comes a new enslavement to righteousness (1 Cor. 6:19-20). For the Christian, ethical standards are not eliminated, rather they are now a goal that can be achieved.

6:19-20. Finally, Paul appeals to them to appropriate the truth of this new life in their daily lives. The appeal is presented as a comparison (*just as...so also*). They should be perfectly obedient slaves to righteousness, just as they were perfectly obedient slaves to sin. *Present your members as slaved to righteousness* reiterates Paul's appeal in Rom. 6:13. This will result in *sanctification*. Sanctification, the state of perfect holiness is the goal of our enslavement to righteousness, not the immediate result. The Christian life is a process of growing in holiness.

6:21-23. Paul closes the section by reminding his readers of the two very different outcomes of slavery to sin and slavery to God. Paul asks them to consider the outcome of their former sinful activities. *The outcome of those things is death.* As elsewhere in the passage, death certainly refers to eternal death. However, even for the Christian we should understand that any sin in our lives is deadly and therefore should be avoided. Clearly there is no *benefit* to sin. On the other hand, there is great benefit to our *enslavement to God.* We gain *sanctification and eternal life.* The Christian life is not an enslavement that eliminates all the benefits of life; it is the very source of what is truly beneficial. Paul reiterates the thought in verse 23. *The wages of sin is death.* Wages, *opsōnion,* is provision money given to purchase food and supplies, often for soldiers (Luke 3:14, 1 Cor.9:7). There is some parallel in the thought to Rom. 4:4 but there Paul uses the word *misthos,* the wage paid for work performed in service to another. For the sinful works performed by those who are not saved, the only remuneration will be eternal death. In contrast, those who accept God's *free gift* gain *eternal life.* Free gift, *charisma,* ties this section back to Rom. 5:15-16 and makes it clear that this life is not on the basis of our obedience or works. This life is a free gift of God's grace and is gained by faith. However, it does not free us from ethical standards. It rather enslaves us to those standards. We should not lose sight of the fact that Paul addresses these things to Christians. We most often use Rom. 6:23 in conjunction with evangelism and rightly we should but we must also consider the purpose of the verse for those who profess faith. As James says, faith without works is dead (Jam 2:17) and cannot truly save. To have faith in

Jesus Christ is to turn from sin and to choose to be a slave of Christ. Those who remove this from faith are liars (1 Jn. 1:6).

Living Under Law Results in Slavery to Sin and Death   *7:1-25*

Summary The Christian is no longer under Law because under Law indwelling sin leads to sinful actions that result in death.

Structural Layout

You were made to die to Law
> that you might be joined to Him raised from dead
> so that we serve in newness of Spirit.

Is the Law sin? Never!
> I would not have known sin except through Law
> But sin produced coveting

So then,
> the Law is holy, righteous, good.

Did that which is good become a cause of death? Never!
> it was sin

For
> Law is spiritual but I am of flesh
> Principle that evil is present in me
> The law of sin which is in my members

So then
> with mind I am serving the Law of God
> with my flesh, the law of sin.

Overview

Paul begins the chapter by stating that the Christian is not under the Law (Rom. 7:1-6). This is necessary because under Law *sinful passions aroused by Law bear fruit for death.* The system of Law is a system characterized by slavery to sin that results in eternal death. This leads to the objection that Paul views the Law as sinful (Rom. 7:7, Rom. 7:13). Paul spends the remainder of the chapter (Rom. 7:7-25) refuting this objection. Paul first argues that sin, not the Law is the cause of my sin and death (Rom. 7:7-12). He concludes his rebuttal with *so then* the Law is holy, and righteous and good (Rom. 7:12).

This leads to the objection that Paul makes Law the cause of death (Rom. 7:13-25). Again, Paul argues that sin, not the Law is the cause of his death. He again affirms the goodness of the Law in Rom. 7:14 and then vividly illustrates that his enslavement to sin leads to sinful acts even though he acknowledges the goodness of the Law (Rom. 7:15-20). He concludes that he is living under the principle of sin and death (Rom. 7:21-24). So, in the end, with his mind he affirms the goodness of the Law but since he is enslaved to sin, he serves sin (Rom. 7:25).

The key to understanding the argument of the chapter is to note that Rom. 7:5, the pre-salvation dynamic of life under Law, is expanded and explained in Rom. 7:7-25 and that Rom. 7:6, the new dynamic of life in the Spirit, is expanded and explained in Rom. 8:1-17. In Rom. 7:5 Paul describes the dynamic of life under Law, a pre-salvation experience *while we were in the flesh*. The flesh refers to the old life that was enslaved to sin. In Rom. 7:6 Paul describes the dynamic of life in the Spirit, the current experience of the saved when he states, *but now we have been released from the Law*.

The Christian is No Longer Under Law   *7:1-6*

¹Or do you not know, brethren (for I am speaking to those who know the law), that the law has jurisdiction over a person as long as he lives? ²For the married woman is bound by law to her husband while he is living; but if her husband dies, she is released from the law concerning the husband. ³So then, if while her husband is living she is joined to another man, she shall be called an adulteress; but if her husband dies, she is free from the law, so that she is not an adulteress though she is joined to another man.

⁴Therefore, my brethren, you also were made to die to the Law through the body of Christ, so that you might be joined to another, to Him who was raised from the dead, in order that we might bear fruit for God. ⁵For while we were in the flesh, the sinful passions, which were aroused by the Law, were at work in the members of our body to bear fruit for death. ⁶But now we have been released from the Law, having died to that by which we were bound, so that we serve in newness of the Spirit and not in oldness of the letter.

Summary   The Christian has died to the Law that bound him to sin and death and is now joined to Christ and serves in the Spirit.

Structural Layout

Law has jurisdiction as long as he lives.
    Married women bound by law
        If her husband dies,
    she is released from the law
free from the Law
    joined to another man

Therefore
    You made to die to Law
    joined to Him who was raised
    bear fruit for God
        For
            While we were in the flesh
        sinful passions by Law
        bear fruit for death
            Now
    we have been released from the Law
        having died to what you were bound
    So that we serve in Spirit

7:1-6 Commentary

The section is divided into two parts. In the first part Paul explains the principle that the Law has jurisdiction over a person only as long as he lives (Rom. 7:1-3). Then Paul applies this principle to the Christian and shows that our death with Christ has released us from the Law (Rom. 7:4-6).

7:1-3. When Paul writes that *the law has jurisdiction over a person as long as he lives*, he is stating that the Law's dominion ends with death (Rom. 7:1). It seems that he must be referring to the Mosaic Law since he says he is *speaking to those who know the Law*, Jews. It would not be logical to think that he is speaking to those who were familiar with basic law such as lawyers.

Paul illustrates this in the law concerning marriage (Rom. 7:2-3). This passage states the general principle that marriage is binding until death (1 Cor. 7:39). However, the passage does not state that there are no exceptions. A general rule may have exceptions. Compare Heb. 9:27 with 1 Thess. 4:17. However, all exceptions must be established in Scripture. In this case, Matt 19:9 and 1 Cor.7:15 may be exceptions though both are highly debated. The idea of being *joined to another* is best understood as being united in marriage. If a woman's husband is alive, to be joined to another would be considered adultery. Yet, if her husband died, she is free to marry another person. Death releases her from the obligation imposed by the Law.

7:4-6. Next Paul applies the principle to the Christian. He draws on our union with Christ and his death much as he did in Rom. 6:1-10. Since we died with Christ, we are free to *be joined another*. To whom were we formerly joined? It must be sin. The imagery of slavery in Rom. 6:16-20 is replaced with the imagery of marriage. This is not to say that marriage is the same as slavery but rather to press the idea of obligation to a relationship. The old marriage to sin is nullified with the result that we can be joined to Christ, him *who was raised from the dead.* Marriage imagery to describe the relationship between Christ and the believer is found elsewhere in the New Testament (Jn. 3:29, Eph. 5:32, Rev. 19:7). This reiterates the thought of Rom. 6:4-5. We have been united with his life and the result is that we can *bear fruit for God.* Paul explains why this change in status was necessary by contrasting the dynamic of the old life with the dynamic of the new life (Rom. 7:5-6).

The dynamic of our old life in union with sin is described in Rom. 7:5. *While we were in the flesh* describes our life before salvation. Paul uses a past tense verse (*were*) and then in the next verse shifts to the present timeframe with the use of *but now.* Paul first describes this former situation as being *in the flesh.* He uses the term to refer to our pre-salvation state (Rom. 8:9), not to a carnal Christian state. The dynamic of this state was that *sinful passion aroused by Law were at work to bear fruit for death.* The dynamic includes three key concepts: sin, Law, and death. Sinful passions describe our depraved nature that was enslavement to sin. It is the *old self* of Rom. 6:5. Such passions were *aroused by Law* in the sense that when confronted by the divine standard of Law, these passions rebelled against God in violent acts of sin, their *fruit* (Rom. 5:20). Such fruit resulted in death. The Greek text reads *by Law (dia nomou*). This reading may lead one to conclude that Paul sees Law as a participant in this evil process. This is not the case as Paul explains in Rom. 7:7-25. Law is the catalyst but clearly not the cause of sins and death. As explained in Rom. 7:8, 11), law provided the opportunity for sin but it did not cause it. In Rom. 8:2 this dynamic of the old life is called *the law of sin and death*.

The new dynamic of life in union with Christ is described in Rom. 7:6. *But now* marks the shift from the description of the pre-salvation life to our current salvation experience. In this new dynamic, *we have been released from the Law*. We are no longer under Law but instead are under grace (Rom. 6:14). We have also died to that by which we were bound. To what were we bound? We were bound to sin (Rom. 6:17) and now we have died to sin (Rom. 6:2). Now *we serve in newness of the Spirit*. Newness echoes back to Rom. 6:4 where Paul describes the Christian as walking in newness of life. Spirit looks forward to Paul's discussion of the empowering work of the Spirit in chapter 8 where the Spirit is referred to at least sixteen times. This new dynamic is *not in oldness of the letter*. It is not the legalistic approach to sanctification found under Law (2 Cor. 3:6).

The Law is holy but cannot overcome indwelling sin 7:7-25

[7]What shall we say then? Is the Law sin? May it never be! On the contrary, I would not have come to know sin except through the Law; for I would not have known about coveting if the Law had not said, "You shall not covet." [8]But sin, taking opportunity through the commandment, produced in me coveting of every kind; for apart from the Law sin is dead. [9]I was once alive apart from the Law; but when the commandment came, sin became alive and I died; [10]and this commandment, which was to result in life, proved to result in death for me; [11]for sin, taking an opportunity through the commandment, deceived me and through it killed me. [12]So then, the Law is holy, and the commandment is holy and righteous and good.

[13]Therefore did that which is good become a cause of death for me? May it never be! Rather it was sin, in order that it might be shown to be sin by effecting my death through that which is good, so that through the commandment sin would become utterly

sinful. ¹⁴For we know that the Law is spiritual, but I am of flesh, sold into bondage to sin.

¹⁵For what I am doing, I do not understand; for I am not practicing what I would like to do, but I am doing the very thing I hate. ¹⁶But if I do the very thing I do not want to do, I agree with the Law, confessing that the Law is good. ¹⁷So now, no longer am I the one doing it, but sin which dwells in me. ¹⁸For I know that nothing good dwells in me, that is, in my flesh; for the willing is present in me, but the doing of the good is not. ¹⁹For the good that I want, I do not do, but I practice the very evil that I do not want. ²⁰But if I am doing the very thing I do not want, I am no longer the one doing it, but sin which dwells in me.

²¹I find then the principle that evil is present in me, the one who wants to do good. ²²For I joyfully concur with the law of God in the inner man, ²³but I see a different law in the members of my body, waging war against the law of my mind and making me a prisoner of the law of sin which is in my members. ²⁴Wretched man that I am! Who will set me free from the body of this death? ²⁵Thanks be to God through Jesus Christ our Lord!

So then, on the one hand I myself with my mind am serving the law of God, but on the other, with my flesh the law of sin.

Summary   Indwelling sin, which dominates me completely, not the Law, is the cause of my sin and death.

Structural Layout

```
Is the Law sin?  Never!
     I would not have known sin except through Law
     sin produced in me coveting of every kin, killed me
So then,
     the Law is holy, righteous, good.
Did that which is good become a cause of death?  Never!
     it was sin
          For
               Law is spiritual but I am of flesh
                    I am doing the very thing I hate
                    Sin which indwells me
                    Principle that evil is present in me
                    The law of sin which is in my members
     So then
          with mind I am serving the Law of God
          with my flesh, the law of sin.
```

7:7-25 Commentary

Paul's statement in Rom. 7:5 that *sinful passions were aroused by the Law* seems to imply that Law is to be blamed for human sinfulness. Does Paul suggest that Law is the agent that urges us to sin? If so, Paul would be implicating Law and implying that it is sinful. This objection is posed and then answered in this section. Paul first argues that sin, not the Law is the cause of my sinful actions and my death (Rom. 7:7-12). He concludes his rebuttal with *so then the Law is holy, and the commandment is holy, righteous and good* (Rom. 7:12).

A second objection is then posed and answered by Paul, namely that Paul makes Law the cause of death (Rom. 7:13-25). Again, Paul argues that sin, not the Law is the cause of his death. He again affirms the goodness of the Law in Rom. 7:14 but does not stop there. What follows in Rom. 7:15-25 is an extended explanation of why he sins in spite of the fact that the Law is spiritual. In contrast to the Law, he is *of flesh* and enslaved to sin. Paul vividly illustrates this enslavement, how it leads to sin even though he acknowledges the goodness of the Law (Rom. 7:15-20). This leads to his ultimate conclusion about his condition. He lives under the principle of sin and death, is wretched, and is enslaved to sin (Rom. 7:21-25a). So, in the end with his mind he affirms the goodness of the Law but since he is enslaved to sin, he serves sin (Rom. 7:25b).

The two units are structured in the same way. They being with a rhetorical question that introduces the objection (Rom. 7:7, Rom 7:13). This is followed by a strong rejection of the objection in the phrase, *May it never be* (*mē ginoito*). Next comes a detailed explanation that sin, not Law, is to blamed for his condition (Rom. 7:8-11, Rom. 7:13-24). The conclusion is introduced by strong inferential markers *so then, hōste* (Rom. 7:12) and *so then, ara oun* (Rom. 7:25). Finally, the goodness of the Law is affirmed (Rom. 7:12, Rom. 7:25).

The first person, used throughout this section, has been variously interpreted. Expositors have suggested four different views.

Paul writes typically of the whole race. Some have suggested that Paul wrote to describe the depravity of the whole world. As such, he speaks about a pre-Christian experience. In this view depravity is defined as an enslavement of the will, not of the heart. Though individuals may want to serve God, they are incapable of doing so. This view was held by some of the early Greek fathers.

Paul writes typically of a legalistic Jew. Some have suggested that Paul wrote to describe the situation in which Jews find themselves under Law. As such, he speaks about a pre-Christian experience. In this view Jews, who looked to the Law for righteousness, completely failed since they were powerless to follow what the Law told them to do. This is the view of most of the early church fathers, the Pietists, and by a minority at the current time.

Paul writes autobiographically. Some have suggested that Paul wrote about his own experiences and restricts the comments to him alone. Those who hold this view see Paul speaking about his Christian experience in the whole passage. Some suggest that he speaks of a time when he still used the Law as a means of sanctification. Others see Paul relating his continual struggle between the old nature and the new nature. This view is held only by a few.

Paul writes about both his Jewish and Christian experience. Paul first writes about his life in Judaism (7:7-13) and then about his Christian experience (7:14-25). Those who hold this view emphasize the shift in tense that occurs at 7:14. This view was followed by most of the reformers and is a common view of many today.

The strongest case can be made for the position that Paul wrote typically of a legalistic Jew. The fact that this individual is struggling under Law would seem to eliminate the view that Paul is speaking typically of the whole race. If as I will argue below Rom. 7:14-25 describes a pre-salvation experience, then the other two views are also eliminated.

7:7-12. In this section, Paul gives his first rebuttal to the objection to his statement in Rom. 7:5, *sinful passions which were aroused by Law*. The words, *by*

Law, could be misconstrued to mean that Law is the agent behind our sinful acts. So, the objection is raised, *Is the Law sin?* The question uses metonymy and should be understood, is the Law the cause of my sin? Paul rejects such an idea in his normal diatribe manner. *May it never be!* He then proceeds to answer the objection. Paul begins by asserting the positive value of Law; it reveals sin (Rom. 7:7). He *would not have come to know sin except through the Law.*

The true agent of our sinfulness is something Paul calls *sin* (Rom. 7:8). Throughout the passage sin is personified. It is always found in the singular and refers not to acts of sin, but to an evil influence in the world. It is not strictly the old nature. Paul views it as something outside himself, which has indwelt and captivated him. Sin *has taken opportunity through the commandment.* That is, sin has used God's commands as the occasion for producing rebellion in the hearts of people (Rom. 7:8, Rom. 7:11).

Paul explains that *apart from Law sin is dead.* If there had been no standard, then outward rebellion would be impossible and sin would have no opportunity. It would be a dead force, lying dormant, having little vitality. He *was once alive apart from the Law* (Rom. 7:9). This is not referring to an historical occasion or to a theological reality. It refers to a personal opinion. In reality Paul was never spiritually alive since he was a sinner from birth (Rom. 5:12). However, without Law sinfulness is not easily known (Rom. 3:20, Rom. 7:7). He thought he was alive. But when confronted by Law, sin caused him to overflow with acts of sin. *Sin became alive and I died.* These external acts made his inner sinfulness quite evident. His opinion of himself was shattered. He realized that he was dead in sin. Sin had killed him. In the end the Law, which was to result in life, *proved to result in death* (Rom. 7:10). Even in this statement Paul puts a positive slant on the Law. It had the divine promise of life (Lev. 18:15). It also had the curse of death (Deut. 30:15).

Paul concludes (Rom. 7:12) that the problem is not with the Law. *The Law is holy, and the commandment is holy and righteous and good.*

7:13-14. In this section, Paul answers a second objection to his statement in Rom. 7:5, *sinful passions which were aroused by Law bear fruit for death.* In Rom. 7:11 when Paul says that sin *through it (Law) killed me*, he indicates that the Law is not the agent but the instrument of his death. Does this imply that the Law caused his death? If so, there must be something evil in Law. So, the objection is raised, *did that which is good become a cause of death for me?* Again, Paul rejects such an idea with the words, *May it never be!* He then proceeds to answer this second objection.

As in Rom. 7:8 Paul blames sin, not Law (Rom. 7:13) for his death. The Law reveals the true nature of sin. By using what was *good* to bring about his death, sin reveals itself to be *utterly sinful*. Paul again affirms the goodness of Law (Rom. 7:14). *The Law is spiritual*. However, he is not spiritual. He is *of flesh*.

Many, especially those from the modern era, suggest that in Rom. 7:14-25 Paul is describing the Christian's struggle with sin. They offer the following arguments.

1. The tense of the verbs shifts from the past tense to the present tense at Rom. 7:14. This must indicate a shift from a past pre-salvation experience (Rom. 7:7-13) to the present salvation experience (Rom. 7:14-25).

2. Paul expresses hatred for sin and a desire to do what is good (Rom. 7:15, Rom. 7:18). These sentiments can only be explained if the individual is saved. The unsaved do not have such desires.

3. The term, *of flesh* (*sarkinos*) in Rom. 7:14 is used to describe a Christian who is not controlled by the Holy Spirit (1 Cor.3:1-4).

4. Rom. 7:14-25 is part of a large context (Rom. 6-8) that is dealing with sanctification. It is only fitting that Paul would discuss the struggle that the Christian has with sin as part of this discussion.

5. The description of Paul's pre-salvation life as a Jew in Philippians 3:4-6 contradicts the description of himself in this passage. Before his salvation Paul was self-righteous and considered himself blameless. In Rom. 7:14-25 he sees himself to be wretched and sinful.

6. The statement, *Thanks be to God through Jesus Christ our Lord* in Rom. 7:25 indicates that Paul is speaking of a Christian.

7. The passage parallels our own experience as Christians in our struggle with sin (Gal. 5:17). Like Paul, the Christian wants to do what is right but often finds that his sinful nature leads him to defeat.

Despite what seems to be strong support, it is more likely that Paul continues to describe a pre-salvation experience, speaking typically as a religiously zealous Jew under the Law. The following reasons support this view.

1. The purpose of the near context (Rom. 7:7-25) is to answer objections to Paul's statement in Rom. 7:5, *While we were in the flesh, sinful passions aroused by Law bear fruit for death.* Rom. 7:5 refers to a pre-salvation experience under Law. In contrast, the Christian is not under Law (Rom. 6:14, Rom. 7:6). Key terms that describe the pre-salvation state in 7:5 are repeated throughout Rom. 7:14-25. These include, flesh, sin, law, death. In contrast, the key term that is associated with the salvation experience described in 7:6, Spirit, is not found in 7:7-25 but is a key term found in Romans 8.

2. The literary structure of the passage requires a break at Rom. 7:13 where the parallel question to Rom. 7:7 is found, not at Rom. 7:14 where the shift in tense is found. The two sections (Rom. 7:7-12 and Rom. 7:13-25) follow the same basic pattern. Each begins with a rhetorical question that raises the objection. Next Paul rejects the objection with the standard *May it never be!* Then he blames sin for his problem and shows that the Law is not culpable. Finally, he states his conclusions that the Law is good. In each instance, the conclusion is marked off with *so then* (*hōste* in Rom. 7:12, *ara oun* in Rom. 7:25). The connector found at 7:14, *for* (*gar*) indicates the development of a closely associated idea, tying what came before closely with what

follows. This marker is not normally used to introduce a new topic or direction.

3. Paul's basic contention, namely that sin not Law is to be blamed for his sinful state, is continued without interruption from Rom. 7:7 to the end of the chapter (Rom. 7:8, Rom. 7:11, Rom. 7:13, Rom. 7:17, Rom. 7:20, Rom. 7:23, Rom. 7:25). This contention is in response to the objection posed in 7:7 and 7:13 to his statement in 7:5 about the dynamic of life before salvation, namely that *sinful passions aroused by Law bear fruit for death.* This statement could be construed to suggest that Paul is blaming the Law for sinful actions. Throughout 7:7-25 he repeatedly states that Law is good and that sin is to be blamed. The Christian is not under Law (Rom. 6:14, Rom. 7:4, 6) and so it seems quite out of place for Paul to include a discussion of Law within a discussion of Christian living.

4. The position of the believer described in chapters six and eight is irreconcilable with the statements made in 7:14-25.

    a. This man is sold under sin (Rom. 7:14) but the believer is freed from sin (Rom. 6:17-22).

    b. This man is in the flesh (Rom. 7:14, Rom. 7:18) but the believer is in the Spirit and not in the flesh (Rom. 7:6, Rom. 8:9).

    c. This man is under the Law (Rom. 7:16) but the believer is released from Law (Rom. 7:6).

    d. This man is unable to do anything good (Rom. 7:18) but the believer is able to serve God (Rom. 6:11-13, Rom. 7:6, Rom. 8:8-9).

    e. This man is a captive to the law of sin and death (Rom. 7:23-24) but the believer is freed from the law of sin and death (Rom. 8:2-3).

5. The contrast introduced by the statement in Rom. 8:1, *There is therefore now no condemnation* is not between two types of Christians, but between the unsaved, those who are condemned (Rom. 7) and the saved, those who are not condemned (Rom. 8). *Now* is commonly employed by Paul in Romans to indicate a shift from the pre-salvation experience to that of the Christian experience (Rom. 5:9, Rom. 6:19, Rom. 6:21, Rom. 6:22, Rom. 7:6).

6. Finally, the arguments offered for the passage referring to the Christian experience can be explained.

   a. The shift from the past tense to the present tense does not necessarily indicate a shift in time. It is just as likely that the shift in tense is rhetorical and indicates a shift in dramatic description. Such use of the present tense is classified as an historic present—a dramatic way to describe past events. This approach is commonly used in the Gospels to bring emphasis or vividness. Paul uses this approach in Rom. 9:27 when he writes, *Isaiah cries out concerning Israel.* Yet, Isaiah spoke hundreds of years before. See also Rom. 10:5, Rom. 10:20, and Rom. 11:2. Clearly in Rom. 7:15-20 Paul is vividly portraying enslavement to sin. This use of dramatic presentation correlates well with the emotional style used elsewhere in the epistle.

   b. The hatred for sin and the agreement with Law expressed in Rom. 7:15-18 correlates perfectly with the sentiments of a religious Jews (Rom. 9:31, Rom. 10:2-3). They were zealous for the Law and were pursuing righteousness. It is incorrect to think that the unsaved cannot desire to do what is good. Enslavement to sin does not mean that people cannot desire to do good, it means that in spite of their desires, they cannot accomplish this good. Even Jesus agreed that evil people can do good (Matt. 7:11).

c.   The use of the term, *of flesh (sarkinos)* in Rom. 7:14 differs from the way it is used in 1 Cor.3:1-4. When the Christians are called *fleshly* in 1 Cor.3:4 Paul uses the term, *sarkikos* meaning flesh-like. When he does use the term, *sarkinos* meaning consisting of flesh in 1 Cor.3:1 he adds the word, *as (hōs)*. In both cases, Paul is comparing the actions of the Corinthians to those of the unsaved. However, he does not directly call them *sarkinos*. They are only like *sarkinos*. They are *sarkikos*. The Corinthians were acting like what they no longer were.

To correctly understand Paul's meaning of flesh in Rom. 7:14, we must see how he defines it within the near context. In Rom. 7:5 Paul describes being *in the flesh* as being in a pre-salvation state. He does the same in Rom. 8:9. To be *in the flesh* is the opposite of being *in the Spirit;* and those who are not in the Spirit are not saved.

d.   Those who see the broader context of Rom. 7:14-25 (Rom. 6-8) as dealing topically with Christian sanctification fail to see that Paul is debating with an imaginary Jew who believes that Law provides the only deterrent to sin. Paul is not providing a practical lesson on sanctification, he is arguing that the system of grace can produce sanctification and that the system of Law cannot. It is this second point that Paul is describing in Rom. 7.

e.   The description given in Rom. 7:14-25 does not contradict Paul's description of himself in Philippians 3:4-6. If this passage is describing Paul's struggle as a

Christian, and Philippians is describing his life as a Jew, we would conclude that Paul was gaining greater victory over sin under Law than he was under grace! In reality, this passage describes what Paul was experiencing on the inside, while Philippians describes Paul's experience on the outside.

f. The statement, *Thanks be to God through Jesus Christ our Lord* in Rom. 7:25 certainly could not be understood as coming from the mouth of an unsaved Jew. Indeed, Paul is speaking as a Christian. However, the statement is parenthetic to the main argument. In his unsaved wretched state, he cries out, *Who can set me free?* (Rom. 7:24). Throughout this discussion, slavery to sin is the state of the unsaved and being set free is the state of the Christian (Rom. 6:18 Rom. 8:22, Rom. 8:2). A Christian would not ask this question. However, at this point Paul the writer cannot hold back the answer. So, he shouts aloud in praise, *Thanks be to God through Jesus Christ our Lord.*

g. Though some statements in the passage seem to parallel our own Christian experience, there are some striking differences. This individual is not struggling in such a way that sometimes he finds victory and other times he finds defeat. This person never finds any victory in his struggle with sin. He is enslaved and imprisoned (Rom. 7:21-23). This passage does not depict a soldier fighting in a battle; it depicts a prisoner, a captive of sin.

7:15-20. Paul expands upon the idea that he is *of flesh* (Rom. 7:14). He explains why he is unable to produce good when confronted with the goodness of the Law. The answer is the domination of sin in his life (Rom. 7:17, Rom. 7:20). The problem is *sin which dwells in me.* He is powerless to accomplish what he desires. Paul describes sin as an external force distinct from his own will. Paul is not attempting to make an excuse for his actions. He is rather attempting to describe the fact that he mentally understood the goodness of the Law and yet he could not obey it. In his mind, he *confesses that the Law is good.* The fact that he *wants to do good* clearly demonstrates that he believes the Law is good.

7:21-25a. In this section, Paul concludes the description given in Rom. 7:15-20 synthesizing it into a single *principle* (*nomos*) that dominates his life *of flesh.* This conclusion is marked off by *then (ara)* (Rom. 7:21). In this instance *nomos* refers to a general controlling principle in life, like the law of gravity is in physics. This principle in general is that *evil is present in me.* He is infected with sin.

Yet this sin does not keep him from *wanting to do good.* Nor does it keep him from acknowledging the goodness of the Law. For he *joyfully concurs with the law of God in the inner man.* To *joyfully concur* means to delight in something or to gain pleasure from something. *In the inner man* refers to one's seat of emotions. *The Law of God* must refer to Mosaic Law since his acknowledgement of the goodness of this Law is a reiteration of his acknowledgement of the goodness of the Mosaic Law issued above (Rom. 7:12, Rom. 7:14, Rom. 7:16). With this statement Paul gives even greater emphasis to his acknowledgement of the goodness of the Law. He has acknowledged it mentally and now he acknowledges it emotionally.

Yet this pervasive principle of indwelling sin is more powerful than both his mind and heart. It *wages war against the law of my mind* (Rom. 7:22). *The law of his mind* is his acknowledgement of the goodness of the Law. The principle of evil within him is directly opposed to his thoughts and emotions. It wages war *making me a prisoner.* In the end, this principle is stronger than that of his mind. It defeats him on every occasion and imprisons him. He is *a prisoner of the law of sin* (Rom. 7:23). Paul entitles this principle, *the law of sin.* In Rom. 8:2 he calls it *the law of sin and death.* This is the same principle that he described in Rom. 7:5 when he said, the *sinful passions, which were aroused by the Law, were at work in the members of our body to bear fruit for death.*

His state is *wretched* and *dead* (Rom. 7:24). In such a miserable state, he cries out for help, *Who will set me free from the body of this death?* Throughout this discussion, slavery to sin is the state of the unsaved and being set free is the state of the Christian (Rom. 6:18 Rom. 8:22, Rom. 8:2). A Christian would not ask this question. It is the unregerate Jew who in total frustration cries out. Yet, Paul, the writer cannot hold back from answering the question. He says, *Thanks be to God through Jesus Christ our Lord!* (Rom. 7:25a). This cannot be considered part of his conclusions since it comes before the *so then* that marks off the conclusion. It fits best with chapter eight and therefore must be considered parenthetic.

7:25b. The two words, *so then*, summon the major conclusion and parallel the conclusion given in Rom. 7:12. Paul begins by affirming the goodness of the Law with the words; *with my mind I am serving the law of God. The law of God* must be the Mosaic Law since throughout the chapter the Mosaic Law has been in view when divine standard is meant (Rom. 7:5, Rom. 7:7, Rom. 7:12, Rom. 7:14, Rom. 7:16, Rom. 7:22). The *mind* does not refer to his regenerated new nature but to Paul's thoughts and desires (Rom. 7:14, Rom. 7:16, Rom. 7:22). He continually acknowledges that the Law is good.

Then Paul blames sin for his failures with the words, *with my flesh the law of sin.* The *flesh*, his enslaved human will (Rom. 7:14), is incapable of doing what his mind desires. Thus, as he concluded in Rom. 7:12, depraved life under Law described in Rom. 7:5 does not suggest that there is anything wrong with Law. Rather it demonstrates how utterly enslaved to sin is the person apart from Christ and how utterly impossible it is to meet the righteous standard revealed in the Law. The Law itself provides no help, no victory for it is weak through the flesh (Rom. 8:3)

The Spirit Brings Victory Over Sin and Death 8:1-39

Summary The Christian, alive by the Spirit, has victory over sin and death, is no longer obligated to the flesh, finds help during suffering, and can be assured of future glory.

Structural Layout

therefore
  There is now no condemnation to those in Christ
    For Law of Spirit of life in Christ has set you free
                                        from law of sin and death
  us who walk according to the Spirit
So, then
  we are under obligation, not to the flesh
    by Spirit putting to death deeds of flesh

the sufferings of this present time are not worthy
    to be compared with the glory that is to be revealed to us.
  For
    the whole creation groans and
    also we groan within ourselves
      having the first fruits of the Spirit,
        waiting eagerly for our adoption as sons

    the Spirit also helps our weakness
    the Spirit Himself intercedes for
    God causes all things to work together for good
  Then,
    what shall we say?
    in all these, we are more than conquerors

Overview

In chapter eight Paul presents the solution to the wretched condition under Law described in chapter seven, expanding upon the thought presented in Rom. 7:6. He presents the believer's new position under grace in contrast to the fruitless struggle of the unsaved under Law in chapter seven. The old dynamic he calls, *the law of sin and death* (Rom. 7:23, Rom. 8:2). The new dynamic he calls, *the law of the Spirit of life in Christ* (Rom. 8:2). This new dynamic is the key to living for God and gaining victory over sin and death.

The chapter deals with our position and is, therefore, true for all Christians. Paul is not talking about the Spirit-filled life as opposed to the life of the carnal Christian. The ministry of the Spirit is not that of filling the believer, but that of permanently indwelling of the believer (Rom. 8:9). The contrast is not between two types of Christians, carnal and spiritual, but between the saved and the unsaved (Rom. 8:1, Rom. 8:8-9, Rom. 8:14). Thus, the section deals with the position and potential of every Christian, not with their actual practice.

In the first section (Rom. 8:1-11), Paul describes the new dynamic, the law of the Spirit of life in Christ. In this dynamic, the Spirit frees the Christian from sin and death and brings the Christian to life through His indwelling presence. From this fact Paul draws the conclusion that the Christian is no longer obligated to the old life but now has freedom in the family of God to live for Him (Rom. 8:12-17).

In the remainder of the chapter (Rom. 8:18-39) Paul handles an objection related to the law of the Spirit of life in Christ. If we have been brought to life, why are we still physically dying and suffering? Paul answers that though we have been given life spiritually, we, like the rest of creation, are still under the curse and are awaiting final deliverance (Rom. 8:18-25). Yet, we do not suffer alone as do the unsaved since we have the help of the Spirit (Rom. 8:26-30). This leads Paul to conclude with confident words of assurance (Rom. 8:31-39).

The Spirit Brings Life   *8:1-11*

¹Therefore there is now no condemnation for those who are in Christ Jesus. ²For the law of the Spirit of life in Christ Jesus has set you free from the law of sin and of death. ³For what the Law could not do, weak as it was through the flesh, God did: sending His own Son in the likeness of sinful flesh and as an offering for sin, He condemned sin in the flesh, ⁴so that the requirement of the Law might be fulfilled in us, who do not walk according to the flesh but according to the Spirit.

⁵For those who are according to the flesh set their minds on the things of the flesh, but those who are according to the Spirit, the things of the Spirit. ⁶For the mind set on the flesh is death, but the mind set on the Spirit is life and peace, ⁷because the mind set on the flesh is hostile toward God; for it does not subject itself to the law of God, for it is not even able to do so, ⁸and those who are in the flesh cannot please God.

⁹However, you are not in the flesh but in the Spirit, if indeed the Spirit of God dwells in you. But if anyone does not have the Spirit of Christ, he does not belong to Him. ¹⁰If Christ is in you, though the body is dead because of sin, yet the spirit is alive because of righteousness. ¹¹But if the Spirit of Him who raised Jesus from the dead dwells in you, He who raised Christ Jesus from the dead will also give life to your mortal bodies through His Spirit who dwells in you.

Summary   The Spirit, who gives us life, has freed us from enslavement to sin and death.

Structural Layout

there is now no condemnation for those who are in Christ Jesus.
For the law of the Spirit of life in Christ Jesus has set you free
from the law of sin and of death.
For
God did what the Law could not do
weak as it was through the flesh,
sending His own Son in the likeness of sinful flesh
He condemned sin in the flesh,
so that the requirement of the Law might be fulfilled in us
who do not walk according to the flesh
but according to the Spirit.
For   the mind set on the flesh is death,
but the mind set on the Spirit is life and peace,
you are not in the flesh but in the Spirit,
if indeed the Spirit of God dwells in you.
If Christ is in you,
though the body is dead because of sin,
the spirit is alive because of righteousness.
if the Spirit of dwells in you,
He will also give life to your mortal bodies
through His Spirit who dwells in you.

8:1-11 Commentary

In this section Paul describes the dynamic under which the Christian lives. He calls it *the law of the Spirit of life*. He contrasts it to the old dynamic, *the law of sin and death*, under which one lives prior to salvation. Thus, he picks up where he left off in Rom. 7:5-6. The description is developed by contrasting these two dynamics and emphasizing the role that the Spirit plays in the new dynamic. The old dynamic was characterized by flesh (Rom. 8:3-8), law

(Rom. 8:3, 4, 7), sin (Rom. 8:2, 3, 10), and death (Rom. 8:2, 6, 10, 11), the same characteristics mentioned in Rom. 7:5. The new dynamic focuses on the role of the Spirit (Rom. 8:2, 4, 9, 11) to produce life (Rom. 8:2, 6, 10-11), also introduced in Rom. 7:6. This new dynamic is *in Christ* (Rom. 8:1, 2, 10), which refers to the believer's union with Christ that resulted in release from enslavement to sin and being alive to God (Rom. 6:1-11).

8:1-2. Paul begins with the victorious statement, *Therefore there is now no condemnation for those who are in Christ Jesus. Now* marks the shift from the pre-salvation discussion of life under Law in chapter seven to the salvation experience of the Christian. Paul moves from the state of wretched condemnation (Rom. 7:24) to the new state of *no condemnation*. This change in status is brought about because of a change in the governing principle of the individual's life. The Christian is now under the *law of the Spirit of life in Christ Jesus*. This is the principle that Paul introduced in Rom. 7:6. This new principle has *set you free from the law of sin and of death*, the principle that dominated life before salvation (Rom. 7:5) and that resulted in condemnation (Rom. 5:8). Just as sin was the power and agent within the old principle (Rom. 7:22-23, Rom. 7:8), so now the Spirit is the power and agent within the new principle. The old principle resulted in death but the new principle results in life (Rom. 6:23).

8:3-4. This new principle is *in Christ Jesus*. He is the one who has accomplished what was necessary to put this principle into effect. It is union with Christ that makes the new dynamic possible (Rom. 6:3-6). The *Law could not do* what was necessary. Though it provided a holy, righteous, and good standard (Rom. 7:12), it required human effort to meet this standard (Rom. 10:2). It was *weak through the flesh*. In contrast *God did* what was necessary *sending His own Son in the likeness of sinful flesh*. Jesus took on flesh and blood and so identified with humanity; he became incarnate (Heb. 2:14). Yet, he was without sin (2 Cor.5:21). He became *an offering for sin*. This short expression summarizes his atoning work described in Rom. 3:24-26. He became our payment for sin. *He condemned sin*. That is, he marked sin for destruction and rendered it powerless (Heb. 2:14).

As a result, *the requirement of the Law might be fulfilled in us*. This requirement is complete and absolute adherence to the standards of the Law (Rom. 2:13; James. 2:10). We fulfill the requirement not in our daily activity, but in our union with Christ through imputed righteousness (Rom. 3:22, Rom. 4:3). Thus, *walking according to the Spirit* must refer to our life in the new dynamic. The unsaved are those who *walk according to the flesh* for they are subject to death (Rom. 8:6), cannot please God (Rom. 8:8), and are still in the flesh (Rom. 8:8).

8:5-8. Paul begins by contrasting the results of life in the flesh with life in the Spirit. Those who *are according to the flesh* are the unsaved. In Rom. 8:9 Paul clearly indicates that those in the flesh are not Christians. Christians are *not in the flesh but in the Spirit*. Those who are according to the flesh *set their minds on the things of the flesh*. They are devoted to sin that has enslaved the flesh (Rom. 7:14) and this sin leads to *death* (Rom. 6:21-23). They are *hostile toward God* because they are *not subject to the law of God*. This summarizes Paul's description of himself in Rom. 7:15-20. The law of God must be the Mosaic Law. Such individuals are living under the law of sin and death. They *cannot please God*.

In contrast, Christians, *who are according to the Spirit*, set their minds *on the things of the Spirit*. They are devoted to the things of God. They have been released from the bondage of sin and now are alive to God (Rom. 6:11), serve in the newness of the Spirit (Rom. 6:7), and bear fruit for God (Rom. 6:4). As a result, they gain *life and peace*. The life is eternal life (Rom. 6:23) and the peace is peace with God (Rom. 5:1).

8:9-11. In Rom. 8:9, Paul turns his attention to the indwelling ministry of the Spirit. The Christian is not *in the flesh but in the Spirit*. To be *in the flesh* is to be living under the dynamic of the old life (Rom. 7:5), which under Law fails to overcome sin because its relies on the impotence of the sin-enslaved flesh. To be *in the Spirit* is to be living under the dynamic of the new life (Rom. 7:6), which under grace employs the power of the Holy Spirit. This new relationship is true because the Spirit *dwells in you*. The Spirit permanently indwells every Christian (John 14:16). Anyone that *does not have the Spirit* does *not belong to Him.* Clearly, Paul is not talking about being filled with the Spirit since the filling of the Spirit is not permanent in the Christian (Eph. 5:18).

When the Spirit indwells a person, He brings that person to life (Rom. 8:10). This is true *though the body is dead because of sin.* Paul is not referring to physical mortality, but to spiritual death (Rom. 7:24). Though we were spiritual dead, the *spirit is alive because of righteousness.* *Spirit* in Rom. 8:10 may refer either to the human spirit or to the Holy Spirit. The contrast between body and spirit supports the idea of human spirit. However, it seems more likely that Paul is describing the Holy Spirit. First, of the 20 instances of spirit in chapter eight only once does Paul speak of the human spirit (Rom. 8:16), and there he clearly distinguishes it with the word, *our.* Second, the word, *alive (zōē),* is the noun, *life,* not the adjective, *alive.* The Holy Spirit is the source of life. Where the Holy Spirit resides, there is life. When the Spirit enters our spiritually dead being, He brings life. The Spirit does this *because of righteousness.* Once by faith we are justified and now gain the righteousness of Christ, it must be that we will be brought to life, for justification leads to life (Rom. 5:17-18).

Paul repeats the thought of bringing the dead sinner to life in Rom. 8:11 but now he attributes this activity to God, the Father. He who *raised Jesus from the dead* refers to the Father. As the Father raised the Son, so he *will give life to your mortal bodies.* As in Rom. 6:5 and Rom. 6:8, the future tense is a future of logical result and refers to our present spiritual regeneration, not to future bodily resurrection. The mention of Christ's resurrection draws us back to our union with Christ (Rom. 6:3-11) where we are united with Christ's life and therefore are alive from the dead. Though we continue to dwell in *mortal bodies,* we are spiritually alive because of the indwelling presence of the Holy Spirit.

One interesting observation should be noted about Paul's description of the Spirit in these verses. In Rom. 8:9 Paul identifies the Spirit as *the Spirit of God.* Then he calls the Spirit, the *Spirit of Christ.* Also in Rom. 8:9 he says the *Spirit of God dwells in you.* Then in Rom. 8:10 he says that *Christ is in you.* All of these terms seem to be used by Paul interchangeably to identify the Holy Spirit and yet they are quite different. These differences indicate an understanding of the trinity. The Holy Spirit is the Spirit of God and at the same time is the Spirit of Christ because Christ is God. When the Holy Spirit indwells the believer, so also Christ dwells in that believer since both are God (Jn. 14:23).

The Spirit Brings Freedom 8:12-17

¹²So then, brethren, we are under obligation, not to the flesh, to live according to the flesh— ¹³for if you are living according to the flesh, you must die; but if by the Spirit you are putting to death the deeds of the body, you will live. ¹⁴For all who are being led by the Spirit of God, these are sons of God.

¹⁵For you have not received a spirit of slavery leading to fear again, but you have received a spirit of adoption as sons by which we cry out, "Abba! Father!" ¹⁶The Spirit Himself testifies with our spirit that we are children of God, ¹⁷and if children, heirs also, heirs of God and fellow heirs with Christ, if indeed we suffer with Him so that we may also be glorified with Him.

Summary   The Spirit has released us from our obligation to the flesh and made us God's adopted children.

Structural Layout

So then
    we are under obligation, not to flesh ---
    For
        if   living according to flesh must die
        if by Spirit   putting to death flesh will live
          by Spirit   led sons of God
          Spirit of adoption
          Spirit bears witness   children of God, heirs

8:12-17 Commentary

So then (ara oun) introduces two implications to the new dynamic of life in the Spirit. First, we are no longer obligated to the flesh (Rom. 8:12-14). Second, we are adopted sons of God (Rom. 8:15-17).

8:12-14. Paul begins by stressing our deliverance from the flesh with the statement; *we are under obligation, not to the flesh.* Christians are not obligated to follow the craving of their human nature. Instead, Christian have a new obligation to live as the slave of God (Rom. 6:18, Rom. 14:8-9; 1 Cor. 6:19-20). Paul does not develop our new obligation, but rather emphasizes our deliverance from the old obligation. This deliverance is essential because *if you are living according to the flesh, you must die.* To live according to the flesh is to live under the old dynamic, the law of sin and death. This results in eternal death. Paul is not implying that Christians can or will live in this condition. He is speaking more axiomatically. The Christian's experience is quite different. Christians are *by the Spirit putting to death the deeds of the body.* In the new dynamic, the Holy Spirit empowers us to holy living. This living is not the means of our justification but the consequence of it. Positionally, we have died to sin in our union with Christ (Rom. 6:2). Practically, we are putting to death sin in our lives (Rom. 6:12-13). Progress in holiness testifies to the deliverance that we have in Christ (1 John 2:3-6). This practical sanctification is possible because we *are being led by the Spirit.* To be led by the Spirit does not refer to daily guidance, but to the encompassing ministry of the Spirit in the life of the Christian (Gal 5:19). As such all Christians are in this way being led by the Spirit and are therefore *sons of God.*

8:15-17. Paul ends the section by developing the idea of being *sons of God.* He describes our new position as sons in God's family and its association with the indwelling Holy Spirit. The Holy Spirit is not *a spirit of slavery leading to fear again.* In the old dynamic, we were enslaved to sin and the result was death. The Holy Spirit is not like that. The Holy Spirit is a *spirit of adoption.* In Greek culture adoption involved the legal act of recognizing an heir who was not a natural son. This heir was given all the rights and privileges of a son. Such adoption often took place when a person had no natural son. Paul uses the term in conjunction with the believer's liberation from the Law in Gal 4:1-5, where he emphasizes the privileges of adoption and distinguishes between the child who, though heir, is still under guardians, and the son, who receives the privileges of adulthood. Similarly, here Paul contrasts a spirit of slavery with the spirit of adoption. Our adoption is liberating and as such we can live free from sin. *The Spirit testifies with our spirit that we are children of God.* The Spirit confirms in our hearts that we are God's children. Yet, this confirmation is not simply a feeling or assurance. The testimony of the Spirit relates to our new freedom from sin and ability to serve God. This new-found obedience is the objective testimony that we are children of God (1 Jn. 2:3, 3:24). As such we are *heirs of God and fellow heirs with Christ.* We inherit the glory of God, His riches, and eternal life.

Paul makes the transition to the next section when he says, *if we suffer with Him.* Does Paul imply a condition upon salvation beyond that of faith? No! His purpose is only to introduce the topic of suffering that he will discuss in Rom. 8:18-30. As the following context will show, this suffering is not suffering that occurs as a result of our choice to follow Christ. It is the natural suffering that besets us because we are a part of this sin-cursed world. Suffering in this way is certain since all will suffer as part of creation. These words, then, are not words of warning. Instead they introduce an objection to Paul's conclusions, as we will see in the following section.

Present Suffering Does Not Refute the Truth of Life in the Spirit   *8:18-30*

¹⁸For I consider that the sufferings of this present time are not worthy to be compared with the glory that is to be revealed to us. ¹⁹For the anxious longing of the creation waits eagerly for the revealing of the sons of God. ²⁰For the creation was subjected to futility, not willingly, but because of Him who subjected it, in hope ²¹that the creation itself also will be set free from its slavery to corruption into the freedom of the glory of the children of God. ²²For we know that the whole creation groans and suffers the pains of childbirth together until now. ²³And not only this, but also we ourselves, having the first fruits of the Spirit, even we ourselves groan within ourselves, waiting eagerly for our adoption as sons, the redemption of our body. ²⁴For in hope we have been saved, but hope that is seen is not hope; for who hopes for what he already sees? ²⁵But if we hope for what we do not see, with perseverance we wait eagerly for it.

²⁶In the same way the Spirit also helps our weakness; for we do not know how to pray as we should, but the Spirit Himself intercedes for us with groanings too deep for words; ²⁷and He who searches the hearts knows what the mind of the Spirit is, because He intercedes for the saints according to the will of God.

28 And we know that God causes all things to work together for good to those who love God, to those who are called according to His purpose. 29 For those whom He foreknew, He also predestined to become conformed to the image of His Son, so that He would be the firstborn among many brethren; 30 and these whom He predestined, He also called; and these whom He called, He also justified; and these whom He justified, He also glorified.

Summary   The Spirit provides us with help and hope during our current sufferings which are a result of the fall and which ultimately work together for our good.

Structural Layout

Sufferings not worthy to be compared to glory to be revealed
For
    creation subjected to futility, slavery to corruption, groans, suffers,
    creation will be set free into glory
And
    we also groan
        having first fruits of Spirit
        waiting adoption as sons, redemption of our body.
Spirit helps our weaknesses, intercedes
All things work together for good
    foreknew, predestined, called, justified, glorified

8:18-30 Commentary

The section is designed to handle an objection to Paul's conclusion that the believer is living under the new dynamic of life in Christ. If it is true that he has been freed from the law of sin and death, and now lives under the law of the Spirit of life, why is he still mortal and why does he suffer? In many ways, this section parallels Rom. 5:1-11 where Paul also discusses Christian suffering. In both we find references to suffering, perseverance, hope, glory, and God's love. The difference is in what prompted each discussion. In Rom. 5 the question was whether current suffering testified against Paul's claim that the Christian is now at peace with God and is assured a glorious future salvation. Here the question is whether current suffering testifies against Paul's claim that the Christian is now by the Spirit's power alive, living under a new dynamic of life in Christ.

Paul answers the objection in three parts. First, he explains that since Christians are part of creation, which remains under God's curse, they will continue in physical suffering and must wait patiently for their final deliverance which will result in the redemption of the physical bodies (Rom. 8:18-25). Next, Paul explains that the indwelling Spirit provides us with help during our sufferings (Rom. 8:26-27). The Spirit intercedes for us in ways of which we would not be capable. Finally, Paul assures his readers that God's eternal plans and purposes will result in our glorification (8:28-30). Though we may not be able to see it, all things are working together toward this ultimate goal.

8:18-25. At the end of verse 17 Paul transitions from the discussion of the law of the Spirit of life in Christ (Rom. 8:2) to a discussion of Christian suffering. This new discussion seems to be based on an objection to Paul's claim that under this new dynamic Christians gain life and freedom from the flesh. If this is true, why do Christians continue to suffer? The assumption is that the physical aspects of this life in Christ will be evident if the spiritual aspects have taken place.

Paul rejects the objection with the statement; *I consider that the sufferings of this present time are not worthy to be compared with the glory that is to be revealed to us.* This is very similar to his positive affirmation about suffering found in Rom. 5:2. Here he distinguishes between two timeframes. The *present time* is the time of the Christians sojourn in this world. This time is characterized by suffering (Job 5:7). This suffering is not suffering that occurs as a result of our choice to follow Christ. As explained in the following verses, it is the natural suffering that besets us because we are a part of this sin-cursed world. The coming age is characterized by *the glory that is to be revealed to us.* Our glorious future is emphasized in the passage (Rom. 8:17, Rom. 8:21, and Rom. 8:30).

He begins his refutation by considering the current state of the created world (Rom. 8:19-22). *The anxious longing of the creation waits eagerly for the revealing of the sons of God. Creation* refers to the natural world of which humanity is part. Using personification, Paul describes it as having a great expectation. *Anxious longing* refers to the straining of the neck in expectation and is used to intensify the idea that *creation waits eagerly*. It is anxiously awaiting *the revealing of the sons of God*. These sons of God are the believers who have been adopted by God (Rom. 8:15-17). At present, there is no physical difference between Christians and non-Christians. This fact is the basis of the objection and so Paul begins his answer by affirming the fact and yet at the same time suggesting that this will not always be the case. The time will come when the difference between believers and non-believers will be revealed.

Paul now explains why creation longs for this time. *Creation was subject to futility*. This refers to the curse that God imposed upon creation when Adam sinned (Gen. 3:17-19). Futility is a state of existence where life is empty, meaningless, and pointless. The book of Ecclesiastes ponders the futility of this world and concludes it is like *striving after the wind* (Ecc. 1:12). Yet, when God imposed the curse, he also offered *hope*. This most likely refers to Gen 3:15 and God's promise that one day this curse would be lifted. On that day, *the creation itself also will be set free from its slavery to corruption into the freedom of the glory of the children of God*. So, the physical or natural aspects of our deliverance will be accomplished only when the curse on the physical world is lifted. This will take place when Christ returns (Rev. 21:1, 22:3). Until that time, creation will continue to *groan and suffer*. Yet this groaning is groaning that is accompanied by hope. Creation groans as a mother in *childbirth*. Though there is pain, there is the hope of delivery and the joy of a birth.

In Rom. 8:23-25 Paul applies this to Christians and concludes that a life of suffering in which physical aspects of our salvation are not yet realized is appropriate for a life of hope. He says that we also *groan within ourselves* because we too are still enslaved to corruption, being part of this creation. Like creation our groaning involves a longing for something better because we have been given a promise of something better. We have *the first fruits of the Spirit*. The Holy Spirit is the first fruits. The Holy Spirit has come into our lives and has given us a taste of heaven and victory over sin and death. So, we long for the fullness. We *wait eagerly for our adoption as sons, the redemption of our body*. We have already been adopted (Rom. 8:14-17) and have already been redeemed (Rom. 3:24). But our adoption and redemption are not yet complete. The physical aspect of these things remains to be accomplished in the future.

Why has this physical aspect of our salvation not yet occurred? It is because *in hope we have been saved.* Salvation is entered into by faith and is lived out in hope. Hope is faith directed at a future object. They work together. *Hope that is seen is not hope.* If God completed our salvation through physical deliverance, there would be no room for hope. Since there remains a part of salvation that we do not see, *with perseverance we wait eagerly for it.*

8:26-27. Additionally, though Christians do suffer as part of creation, our new relationship in the law of the Spirit of life in Christ does make a difference. The Spirit who indwells us provides us with help. *The Spirit helps our weakness.* That is, the Spirit provides help in times of suffering. Weakness does not refer to moral or spiritual weakness, but to physical weakness. *We do not know how to pray as we should.* During times of suffering we are to pray (James 5:13); but we do not always know how we should pray. *The Spirit intercedes for us with groanings too deep for words.* This intercession should not be equated with speaking in tongues. Indeed, the prayer associated with speaking in tongues is not intercession but praise and thanksgiving (1 Cor 14:16, Acts 2:11). Paul describes a mind-to-mind, non-verbal communication between the Father and the Spirit. The Father *knows what the mind of the Spirit is.*

8:28-30. He ends by assuring his readers that God is in total control and that his purpose is to bring us to glory. He *causes all things to work together for good.* God uses all things to accomplish His plan. Even suffering and evil ultimately are used to bring about God's ultimate good. Yet this good is directed *to those who love God, to those are called according to His purpose.* God's goodness is directed toward God's people. These are the ones who have freely expressed their love for him and the one's that He has sovereignly chosen. Paul sees no conflict between human freedom and divine sovereignty.

Paul lists God's sovereign activities to emphasize his absolute control over our destiny. First, he *foreknew* us. Calvinists understand foreknowledge as basically equivalent to election. God chose to enter into a relationship with the elect. He fore-loved them. Arminians understand foreknowledge as the basis by which God elected. He foresaw faith in some and on that basis elected them. Either understanding is possible in this context. *He also predestined* us *to become conformed to the image of His Son.* Calvinists understand predestination to be a decree of God in which he determined the eternal fate of every person. The elect are predestined to eternal life and the non-elect are predestined to eternal death. Arminians also understands predestination as pointing to two destinies, either eternal life or eternal death. However, they understand predestination to be God's decision of destinations, not God's decision about who will have that destiny. The choice of destiny is determined by the individual and only foreknown by God. The destiny of those he foreknew is *to become conformed to the image of His Son.* Christians are destined to be like Christ. He is the *firstborn among many brethren.* This points to his resurrection and exultation. He is now crowned with glory and honor and is bringing many sons to glory (Heb. 2:9-10). *He also called* us. Calvinists distinguish between a general external call to all people and a special efficacious call to the elect. This special call is accompanied by irresistible grace. The individual given this call must respond since it is God who is saving him. Arminians see the distinction, not in the calling, but in the response. Those who by faith respond to the call are saved. For them it is an effectual call. Those who reject the call are lost. Those who accept the call respond with the help of prevenient grace. However, this grace can be resisted. The individual can reject God's gift. Paul must be referring to an effectual call in the lives of believers since those *whom He called, He also justified.* This points to the present condition of Christians. We stand justified by faith (Rom. 5:1). One thing remains. Those *whom He justified, He also glorified.* Paul expresses this with the aorist tense that in the indicative normally refers to a past action. However, glory is something yet future (Rom. 8:18). In the mind of God, who has determined our future, glorification has already taken place. It is as good as done.

It is not Paul's point to resolve the theological tensions between Calvinism and Arminianism. Paul is content to mention the timeless activities of God to assure us of God's absolute control of our destiny. In spite of current suffering, we can be assured that we will one day be in glory.

Hymn of Final Assurance   *8:31-39*

31What then shall we say to these things? If God is for us, who is against us? 32He who did not spare His own Son, but delivered Him over for us all, how will He not also with Him freely give us all things? 33Who will bring a charge against God's elect? God is the one who justifies; 34who is the one who condemns? Christ Jesus is He who died, yes, rather who was raised, who is at the right hand of God, who also intercedes for us.

35Who will separate us from the love of Christ? Will tribulation, or distress, or persecution, or famine, or nakedness, or peril, or sword? 36Just as it is written, "For Your sake we are being put to death all day long; We were considered as sheep to be slaughtered." 37But in all these things we overwhelmingly conquer through Him who loved us. 38For I am convinced that neither death, nor life, nor angels, nor principalities, nor things present, nor things to come, nor powers, 39nor height, nor depth, nor any other created thing, will be able to separate us from the love of God, which is in Christ Jesus our Lord.

Summary   Since God has done so much for us, we are surely victors in Christ and that nothing can separate us from His love.

Structural Layout

What shall we say to these things?
　　God is for us who is against us?
　　He spared not His own Son will He not give us all things?
　　God justifies who brings charge?
　　Christ died, raised who condemns?
　　Who shall separate us from love of Christ?
In all these things
　　we overwhelmingly conquer
　　　　through Him who loved us.

8:31-39 Commentary

8:31-34. Paul concludes his rebuttal to the objection with the poetic crescendo of a hymn of faith. The section begins with a series of rhetorical questions that provide complete assurance about God's work for us (Rom. 8:31-34).

There is no opposition.   8:31

There is no limitation.   8:32

There is no accusation.   8:33

There is no condemnation.   8:34

The conclusion begins with the rhetorical question, *what then shall we say to these things?* Though some believe Paul is speaking broadly about God's work presented in Romans, it is more likely that Paul is referring to the list of God's eternal activities given in Rom. 8:28-30. These certainly indicate that *God is for us.* He is on our side. If this is so, then no one can be *against us.* Opposition will come, but no opposition will be able to thwart God's work. The next rhetorical question demonstrates the ideas that God is for us and that our future is secured. He *did not spare His own Son, but delivered Him over for us all.* God has given us His very best. This is the ultimate demonstration of God's love for us (1 John 4:10) and parallel the *a fortiori* argument Paul used in Rom. 5:6-11. If he has already given us His best, then certainly He will *free give us all things.* We will gain the inheritance associated with our adoption (Rom. 8:17) and that will include the redemption of our bodies (Rom. 8:23).

Rom. 8:33-34 can be punctuated in different ways. It seems best to do so in a way that retains the two-clause sets found in Rom. 8:31-32. I would punctuate the material as follows:

> [33]*Who will bring a charge against God's elect? God is the one who justifies.* [34]*Who is the one who condemns? Christ Jesus is He who died, yes, rather who was raised, who is at the right hand of God, who also intercedes for us.*

The two clauses in Rom. 8:33 form a question and response pair and the two clauses in Rom. 8:34 form another question and response pair. To *bring a charge* refers to taking legal action against someone (Acts 19:38). Such a charge against God's elect is impossible because *God is the one who justifies.* God has already made a judicial declaration. He has declared that the elect are not guilty. He has declared them righteous. Similarly, Paul asks, *who is the one who condemns?* To condemn is to render a verdict of guilty. No one can render such a verdict against us because *Christ Jesus is He who died, yes, rather who was raised.* This echoes Paul words in Rom. 4:25. The payment for our sin has been made and accepted by the Father. We no longer are under condemnation (Rom. 8:1). Now that Christ lives, we are being saved by His life (Rom. 5:10) and He continually intercedes for us before the Father as our Great High Priest (1 John 2:1-2, Heb. 4:14).

8:35-39. The series ends with a final rhetorical question by which he declares that there is also no separation from God's love demonstrated in Christ (Rom. 8:35-39). He begins by asking, *who will separate us from the love of Christ* and ends with the confident declaration that nothing *will be able to separate us from the love of God.* Between these two, Paul lists potential advocates first in Rom. 8:35 and then in a rhetorical crescendo in Rom. 8:38-39. He acknowledges that such adversaries exist; but quoting from Psalm 44:22, he shows that such adversaries have always been present among the elect of God. The focal point of the verses is found in Rom. 8:37. *In all these things we overwhelmingly conquer through Him who loved us.* As in Rom. 5:1-11 it is God's love that assures us of our victory. We are completely and overwhelmingly victorious.

Answering the Jewish Covenantal Objection   9:1-11:36

Summary   Justification by faith does not contradict the election of Israel, for God will fulfill His promises to Israel by faith while at the same time rejecting the majority of Jews who fail to believe.

Structural Layout

It is not as though the word of God has failed.
> They are not all Israel who descended from Israel
> Israel did not arrive at law
> They did not pursue it by faith
> A disobedient and obstinate people

God has not rejected His people, has He?
> A remnant according to God's gracious choice
> All Israel will be saved.

113

Overview

In chapters nine through eleven, Paul handles the last major objection to justification by faith, namely that this doctrine contradicts God's election of Israel. If it does, Paul would then be charged with teaching that God does not keep His word. If Paul's teaching does not contradict God's promise to Israel, how can Paul explain Israel's condemnation and current rejection?

This objection is based on two false assumptions. First, that God's election of Israel implies that God had elected individual Jews. Secondly, that the condemnation of individual Jews implies that God had abandoned His promises to the nation of Israel as a whole. To properly understand Paul's argument, one must note the distinction between national and individual election. National election involves God's choice of the nation of Israel as the nation through which God would bring salvation. God made promises in connection with this national election. He promised Israel a kingdom and a future (Rom. 11:26-28). Individual election involves God's choice of individuals for salvation and eternal life. The Jews falsely assumed that since they were a part of the elect nation (physical descent), they were themselves elect (Matt. 3:9; Jn. 8:39).

Paul begins by proving that God has not failed to keep His Word when He rejects individual Jews, since only a small portion of the physical descendants are actually part of God's elect (Rom. 9:1-29). He then demonstrates that their rejection is based on their own unbelief (Rom. 9:30-10:21). Finally, he argues that God is and will fulfill His promises concerning national election (Rom. 11:1-36).

God's Election Not Based on Physical Descent But Divine Mercy   *9:1-29*

Summary The rejection of individual Jews does not contradict God's promise to Israel since not all of the physical descendants were chosen to receive the promises, a merciful choice that is not unjust but clearly within God's rights.

Structural Layout

        Israelites, to whom belongs adoption, glory, covenants, Law, promises
But
        Word of God has not failed
            for
                they are not all Israel who are descended from Israel

    Injustice with God?
        I will have mercy on whom I have mercy
        Potter has right over clay

  God endured with much patience vessels of wrath
        to make known riches upon vessels of mercy

        He says in Hosea
            Not My People
            My People
        Isaiah cries out
            concerning Israel
            the remnant will be saved.

Overview

Paul introduces the objection by affirming his claim that his brothers, the Jews are condemned and by outlining the wealth of Jewish advantages (Rom. 9:1-5). This would logically lead to the question, "How can they be accursed and at the same time have such advantages?" In Rom. 9:6 he responds that these things do not suggest that God has failed to keep His word to Israel since not all of the physical descendants of Israel are part of the elect Israel. In Rom. 9:7-13 he proves the point by demonstrating through the children of Abraham and Isaac that not all physical Jews were chosen by God to receive the promises.

Paul's use of the example of Esau and Jacob leads to the charge that such an election program would be unjust (Rom. 9:14-18). Paul answers that God's election program is not based on justice but on mercy and, as such, God is free to do whatever He desires.

This leads to the charge that such an election program is fatalistic and therefore God has no right to find fault (Rom. 9:19-24). Paul rejects the idea and uses the illustration of the potter to argue that God has the sovereign right to elect whomever He chooses. His patience with Jews, whom Paul calls vessels of wrath, does not negate the fact that they are rejected. He has chosen vessels of mercy, God's elect, from among Jews and Gentiles.

Paul ends the section with Old Testament quotations, first from Hosea to support his claim that Gentiles are included in God's election program, and then from Isaiah to support his claim that only a small portion of the individuals within the nation of Israel are chosen (Rom. 9:25-29).

The Privileges of Israel   *9:1-5*

¹I am telling the truth in Christ, I am not lying, my conscience testifies with me in the Holy Spirit, ²that I have great sorrow and unceasing grief in my heart. ³For I could wish that I myself were accursed, separated from Christ for the sake of my brethren, my kinsmen according to the flesh, ⁴who are Israelites, to whom belongs the adoption as sons, and the glory and the covenants and the giving of the Law and the temple service and the promises, ⁵whose are the fathers, and from whom is the Christ according to the flesh, who is over all, God blessed forever. Amen.

Summary   Paul expresses his grief for the Jewish people and reviews their privileged position with God.

Structural Layout

I have great sorrow and unceasing grief.
I could wish myself accursed for my kinsmen

Who are

Israelites	adoption	glory
covenants	Law	temple service
promises	fathers	Christ

9:1-5 Commentary

9:1-3. Paul begins the section by declaring his *great sorrow* for Israel. The expression of sorrow is meant to dispel any notion that Paul writes from

116

bitterness or malice towards his own people. He has *great sorrow and unceasing grief in* his *heart*. He loves his people. The superlatives, *great* and *unceasing* express an intense longing. He says, *I could wish that I myself were accursed. Accursed (anathema)* involves a judgment that comes as the result of failure to keep an oath or obligation. It is here associated with the judgment that is upon the Jewish because of their condemnation (1 Cor. 16:12, Gal. 1:8-9). He would take on their condemnation if it were possible; but it is not. This, however, does affirm Paul's contention that Jews are condemned (Rom. 3:9).

9:4-5. Next Paul prepares the stage for a new objection to justification by faith by outlining the wealth of Jewish advantages. He takes up the thought begun in Rom. 3:1-2. The Jews have many advantages. Paul does not deny it. Paul lists nine advantages. The first is that they are *Israelites*. All 13 occurrences of the terms, Israel and Israelite, are found in chapters 9-11. It defines the Jews as descendants of Israel who is heir to the promise of Abraham (Rom. 9:10-13). As such, the title takes on theological significance. Second, to them belongs *the adoption as sons and the glory*. These items, adoption, sonship, and glory, Paul mentioned in chapter eight where he described them with reference to the church (Rom. 8:15, Rom. 8:18, Rom. 8:21, Rom. 8:30). These were originally given to Israel. They were the Lord's first-born son (Ex 4:22). The glory of the Lord filled the tabernacle and the temple (Ex 40:34; Ezek. 1:28). They also were given the *covenants*. By this Paul most likely means all the covenants of the Old Testament (Eph. 2:12), including the Abrahamic and Davidic covenants that included distinct promises. They were given the *Law and the temple service*. These most likely refer to the whole Levitical system, including the sacrifices. It is especially important to notice that Paul includes *the promises*. God gave Israel eternal promises. They had the examples of the *fathers* and were privileged to be the race from whom came the *Christ*. The last expression, *God, blessed forever* if so punctuated proclaims that Christ is God. This reading is the reading of all ancient translations, was accepted by the majority of Greek Church fathers, and is preferred by most scholars. The Greek text reads, ὁ ὢν ἐπι πάντων θεὸς εὐλογντὸς, *God*, θεὸς *(theos)*, is in the nominative case and most likely is functioning as a predicate nominative to the adjectival participle, ὢν, translated with the relative clause *who is*. As such the noun is most likely qualitative, having an adjectival force. So, it could be translated, *who is over all, divine, blessed forever*. Since Paul acknowledges only one divine being, this is equal to declaring that Christ is God (Jn. 1:1). If Paul had intended to state only that Christ is God-blessed, he would have used the genitive case instead of the nominative case.

For God to be faithful, He must keep His promises and be faithful to these privileges. The list is impressive. Israel has much going for it. How can God condemn and reject them? Won't their privileges lead to their escape from judgment (Rom. 2:3)? Otherwise God would fail to keep His promises to them. This is the question that Paul will now answer.

The Privileges Limited to the Elect within Israel   *9:6-13*

⁶But it is not as though the word of God has failed. For they are not all Israel who are descended from Israel; ⁷nor are they all children because they are Abraham's descendants, but: "through Isaac your descendants will be named." ⁸That is, it is not the children of the flesh who are children of God, but the children of the promise are regarded as descendants. ⁹For this is the word of promise: "At this time I will come, and Sarah shall have a son." ¹⁰And not only this, but there was Rebekah also, when she had conceived twins by one man, our father Isaac; ¹¹for though the twins were not yet born and had not done anything good or bad, so that God's purpose according to His choice would stand, not because of works but because of Him who calls, ¹²it was said to her, "The older will serve the younger." ¹³Just as it is written, "Jacob I loved, but Esau I hated."

Summary   God has not failed to keep His promises to Israel, for not all the physical descendants were chosen to receive the promises.

Structural Layout

It is not as though the Word of God has failed.
    For
        They are not all Israel who are descended from Israel
            "Through   Isaac   (not Ishmael)" *Gen. 21:12*
                   children of promise   children of flesh
          "Sarah will have a son" *Gen. 18:10*
        Also "The older (Esau) will serve younger (Jacob)" *Gen. 25:23*
             twins, unborn, done nothing good or bad
          so that God's purpose according to His choice
                       not because of works
            because of Him who calls

9:6-13 Commentary

Paul begins by stating that the condemnation and judgment of his own people, the Israelites (Rom. 9:3) does not lead to the conclusion that God has failed to keep his word to them since not all of the physical descendants of Israel are part of the chose nation of Israel. He then provides scriptural evidence related to the descendants of Abraham and Isaac (Gen. 21:12 and Gen. 25:23) to prove that this is true.

9:6. Paul's statement, *But it is not as though the word of God has failed*, is the key proposition in the chapter and is his response to those who claim that his teaching implies that God is unfaithful to Israel. God has not failed to keep His promises to Israel even when he condemns the Jews for their sins. But how can God reject the Jews and yet be faithful to His promises to Israel? The answer Paul explains is that *they are not all Israel who are descended from Israel*. We must distinguish between individual Jews and the nation of Israel. Paul's first instance of the word, *Israel* refers to the elect nation to whom God made the promises listed in Rom. 9:4-5. The second instance of *Israel* refers to the patriarch, Israel. Thus, not all of the physical descendants of the patriarch should be considered part of spiritual Israel, the elect nation to whom He gave the promises. God is free to reject those Jews who are not a part of the elect nation, since they were never given the promises to start with. In rejecting them He is not failing to keep His word.

119

9:7-9. Such an idea, namely that some Jews are not to be included among the elect of Israel, would be shocking to Paul's Jewish opponent. The Jews were quick to claim that their spiritual privilege was based on their physical descent (Matt 3:9, John 8:39). So, Paul must now prove his claim. He does so by considering the earliest descendants, the sons of Abraham and the sons of Isaac, showing that in both cases not all the physical descendants were chosen to receive the promise. He begins with Ishmael and Isaac, quoting Gen. 21:12, *"through Isaac your descendants will be named"*. Sarah, Abraham's wife, was unable to have children. So, Sarah convinced Abraham to bear a child through Hagar, her Egyptian servant girl. Abraham did so and Hagar bore him Ishmael (Gen. 16). Paul describes this as an act of *the flesh*. It directly contradicted God's plan. In Gen. 18:9-14 the Lord promised that Sarah would have a son. Finally, the Lord fulfilled his promise to Sarah and she and Abraham bore Isaac (Gen. 21:1-8). However, this led to bitter jealousy between the two women. Sarah turned against Hagar, demanding that Abraham throw her and her son out. Greatly distressed because he must have loved them both, Abraham turned to the Lord for advice. He must have been surprised at the Lord's advice. The Lord told him to do as Sarah had demanded and cast out Hagar and Ishmael. This, the Lord explained, was because *"through Isaac your descendants will be named."* Cleary, in this case not all the physical descendants were to inherit the promises to Abraham. Paul concludes, it was *not the children of the flesh who are the children of God.* The children of the flesh are the physical descendants and may have some reference to the fact that Ishmael was born, not as part of the promise of God but rather through a fleshly attempt to produce a son. There may also be here an allusion to being in the flesh as described in the old pre-salvation dynamic (Rom. 7:5, 14, 8:3-10). Instead *the children of the promise are regarded as descendants.* These are the spiritual Israelites who will inherit the promises.

9:10-13. The example of Ishmael and Isaac seems weak. First, the two sons had different mothers. Second, the birth of Ishmael was clearly an act of the flesh and not a part of God's promise. So, Paul provides a second example. *There was Rebekah also, when she had conceived twins by one man, our father Isaac.* In this example both sons, Esau and Jacob, were within the godly line, both had the same parents. Indeed, they were twins. Paul also mentions that they *were not yet born and had not done anything good or bad*. Yet, God chose Jacob to receive the promise and rejected Esau. God told Rebekah, *The older will serve the younger* (Gen 25:23). This goes against the cultural standard of the day in which the oldest son would gain the birthright.

Rebekah received this message from the Lord before the twins were born. Paul concludes from this that God chose *not because of works* but *so that God's purpose according to His choice would stand*. Clearly, divine election is not based on works. However, Paul's statement does not indicate that election is arbitrary. It is purposeful. Choosing on the basis of faith would not contradict this concept. For faith is impossible apart from God's call and grace.

Paul concludes the example by quoting from Malachi 1:2-3, *Jacob I loved, but Esau I hated*. This is an example of anthropopathism, speaking of God in terms of human emotions. Hatred is not to be equated with human hatred but with a description of rejection. Love is equated with God's choice. So, we could paraphrase it as saying, "Jacob I have chosen, but Esau I have rejected."

God's Election is Based on Mercy, not Justice   9:14-18

14What shall we say then? There is no injustice with God, is there? May it never be! 15For He says to Moses, "I will have mercy on whom I have mercy, and I will have compassion on whom I have compassion." 16So then it does not depend on the man who wills or the man who runs, but on God who has mercy. 17For the Scripture says to Pharaoh, "For this very purpose I raised you up, to demonstrate My power in you, and that My name might be proclaimed throughout the whole earth." 18So then He has mercy on whom He desires, and He hardens whom He desires.

Summary   There is no injustice in God's election since His election is based on mercy, not on justice.

Structural Layout

> There is no injustice with God, is there?   Never!
>> I will have mercy on whom I have mercy   *Exodus 33:19*
>> Does not depend on man, but on God who has mercy
>> He has mercy on who He desires, hardens whom He desires.

9:14-18 Commentary

Paul's final example of the election of Jacob and rejection of his twin brother, Esau could lead to a charge of injustice with God. Paul counters this idea by showing through Scripture (Ex. 33:19) that divine election is a matter of mercy, not justice and as such God can choose whomever He desires without any loss of His justice.

9:14. The rhetorical questions that begin Rom. 9:14 again introduce a supposed objection to Paul's argument. *What shall we say then? There is no injustice with God, is there?* The idea that God chose one son over another when they were still in the womb and had done nothing wrong seems to make God unjust. Paul rejects this idea in his normal fashion, *May it never be!*

9:15-16. He answers the objection by quoting Exodus 33:19, *I will have mercy on whom I have mercy, and I will have compassion on whom I have compassion.* Paul is claiming that God's election is not a matter of justice but of mercy. Justice involves giving a person what is rightly deserved. A common concept of mercy is that it involves not giving someone what is deserved. This is not the case. Mercy involves responding to a need apart from any righteous demand to do so. The needy cried out to Jesus, *Have mercy on us, Son of David! (Matt. 9:27).* In this case, the need is for salvation and suggests human sin and its consequence -- condemnation. If God responded to us with justice, then we would be condemned to eternal death. Rather God responds to us with compassion and mercy (Rom. 11:30-32, 1 Tim. 1:13, 1 Pet. 2:10).

Paul concludes that God's election *does not depend on the man who wills or the man who runs.* If God's choice were based on merit, He would be required to select those who qualify as a matter of justice. This was Paul's point in Rom. 4:4. However, since no one qualifies as a matter of justice (Rom. 2:23), God's choice is based on His compassion and mercy, and therefore is without any constraint. He is free to choose any, all, or no one without being unjust. No one can demand that God select him or her, not the person who desires eternal life, nor the person who works for eternal life. God is free to do whatever He desires. Does this imply that God selected arbitrarily, apart from foreknowledge, without criteria? No. Paul does not state how God chose, only that He was free to choose in any way He desired, since the choice was not based works (Rom. 9:11). Does the fact that election does not *depend on the man wo wills* eliminate faith as a possible criterion for election? No. It simply means that no one can demand that God elect them, not even a person who has faith. Foreseen faith may have been the criterion by which God freely chose, but deciding on such a criterion is a matter of God's sovereignty, not on human desire.

9:17-18. Paul continues to support the idea that God is free to choose whomever He desires, but now Paul considers those whom God does not choose. Along with selecting some for salvation, God also *hardens* others, that is, He rejects them for salvation and leaves them to their own doings. Paul begins by quoting Ex. 9:16 concerning Pharaoh, *"For this very purpose I raised you up, to demonstrate My power in you, and that My name might be proclaimed throughout the whole earth."* The story of the exodus (Ex. 4-14) does not indicate that God forced Pharaoh to reject God's demand. The narrative does state that God harden Pharaoh's heart (Ex. 4:21, 7:3, 9:12, 10:20, 10:27, 11:10, 14:8). However, it also states that Pharaoh hardened his own heart (8:15, 8:32, 9:34). In addition, there are several occasions where the passive, *was hardened* is used with no agent expressed (Ex. 7:13, 7:22, 8:19, 9:7, 9:35). If God was first to harden Pharaoh's heart, there would seem to be little room left for Pharaoh to harden his own heart. However, if the hardening began with Pharaoh, God could certainly add to it. God had sent six plagues upon Egypt but Pharaoh would not relent. The Lord issued Pharaoh an ultimatum, either let the Israelites go or He would send the full force of His plagues against him. God could have struck the Egyptians down and wiped them from the face of the earth. However, this would not fit into God's plan. God raised Pharaoh up so that He might demonstrate His power and that His name might be proclaimed. What hardened Pharaoh's heart? When his magicians replicated the miracle of turning a staff into a serpent (Ex. 7:13), and when they replicated the miracle of turning the waters of the Nile blood red (Ex. 7:22), Pharaoh hardened his heart. When God relented from a plague, Pharaoh hardened his heart (Ex. 8:15, Ex. 9:34). So, clearly God used various situation to bring about this hardening.

Does the hardening of Pharaoh imply that God thwarted his human will and kept him from believing? No. In Ex. 8:15, Ex. 8:32, and Ex. 9:34 Pharaoh hardened his own heart. God does not manipulate the will to keep a person from responding in obedience and faith. He simply takes away the opportunity where there is rejection (Matt. 13:10-16). This is similar to God's response to Gentile rejection of Him in Rom. 1:24-28. Hardening is a judgment upon those who choose not to believe.

Paul concludes, So *then He has mercy on whom He desires, and He hardens whom He desires.* Divine election involves a sovereign choice that is sources in God's compassion and mercy. There is no demand that God choose someone. Instead, he can simply give people over to their own devices, a judicial act of hardening. God is therefore free to choose whomever He desires for His own glory and grace (Eph. 1:4-6).

God's Election Cannot Be Challenged   *9:19-24*

[19]You will say to me then, "Why does He still find fault? For who resists His will?" [20]On the contrary, who are you, O man, who answers back to God? The thing molded will not say to the molder, "Why did you make me like this," will it? [21]Or does not the potter have a right over the clay, to make from the same lump one vessel for honorable use and another for common use?

[22]What if God, although willing to demonstrate His wrath and to make His power known, endured with much patience vessels of wrath prepared for destruction? [23]And He did so to make known the riches of His glory upon vessels of mercy, which He prepared beforehand for glory, [24]even us, whom He also called, not from among Jews only, but also from among Gentiles.

Summary   God's election cannot be challenged since God has the right to do as He pleases in rejecting Jews and selecting Gentiles.

Structural Layout

> You will say...
>> Why does He find fault?
>> Who resists His will?
> On contrary
>> Who are you to answer back
>> Molded will not say to molder
>> Potter has a right over the clay.
> Endured with patience vessels of wrath (Jews)
> make known glory upon vessels of mercy (Jews & Gentiles)

9:19-24 Commentary

Paul's claim that God is free to elect whomever he desired since God is totally sovereign in his election, either having mercy or hardening, leads to another object, namely that such an election program leads to fatalism and fatalism would remove personal responsibility so that God could not judge individuals for their actions. Paul evades the question, using an illustration of a potter and clay, by simply stating that humans have no right to question God's sovereign choices.   He then explains that God's patience with unbelieving Israelites, whom he calls *vessels of wrath*, does not negate his rejection of them. He was patient with them, not because they were elect, but so that he could make known salvation to those he had chosen, whom he called *vessels of mercy*, made up of both Jews and Gentiles.

9:19. With the words, *You will say to me then,* Paul once again returns to a singular form of *you*. This objection must come directly from his Jewish opponent. *Why does He still find fault? For who resists His will?* The notion that God sovereignly has mercy on some and hardens others leads to the charge that such an election program is fatalistic and therefore God has no right to find fault. This is due to a misunderstanding of divine election. The assumption is that election is deterministic of human actions. This need not be the case. In fact, all election is based on the presupposition of sin and must, therefore, be understood to some degree as conditioned.

9:20-21. Paul rejects the objection and uses the illustration of a potter to argue that God has the sovereign right to elect whomever He chooses. With the question, *who are you, O man, who answers back to God?* Paul describes the great distance there is between God and man. He increases the thought of this distinction when he compares *the thing molded* with *the molder.* The point of the illustration is that God is sovereign over his creation for God has the *right over the clay* to do with it as He chooses. The illustration refers to God's work in electing, not to his work in creating. God did not create individuals so as to make them sinful or unbelieving. What God created was good, very good (Gen. 1:31). He cannot act in a way that is contrary to His own holiness. Election involves God's choice to be gracious to sinners. In this God has total and absolute freedom and sovereignty. In the end, man has no right to challenge God's actions (Job 9:1-12). So, God is free *to make from the same lump one vessel for honorable use and another for common use.* He is free to elect some for salvation and reject others.

9:22-23. Paul now explains God's patient dealing with unbelieving Jews in the past. The question that begins Rom. 9:22 can be summarized, "Why, if many Jews were not elect, was God patient with them? The phrasing of the participle, *although willing to demonstrate His wrath and to make His power known*, is designed to parallel the quotation from Ex. 9:16 found in Rom. 9:17. God had been patient with Pharaoh but his patience was so that His name might be proclaimed throughout the whole earth. Certainly, there was no sense that this patience was a sign of divine favor. So it is with the *vessels of wrath.* These vessels represent the physical descendants of Abraham that were not chosen to be part of spiritual Israel. The idea that divine patience does not suggest escape from judgment is also seen in Rom. 2:4. His patience with unbelieving Jews does not imply that they are elect, but rather is explained as necessary so that God could *make known the riches of His glory upon vessels of mercy, whom He also called, not from among Jews only, but also from among Gentiles.* God has chosen both Jews and Gentiles to receive mercy and gain the riches of His glory. The nation of Israel was a key instrument used by God to communicate His saving message to the world.

Scripture Supports God's Choice of Gentile and Rejection of Jews

9:25-29

²⁵As He says also in Hosea, "I will call those who were not My people, 'My people,' And her who was not beloved, 'beloved.' " ²⁶"And it shall be that in the place where it was said to them, 'you are not My people,' There they shall be called sons of the living God." ²⁷Isaiah cries out concerning Israel, "Though the number of the sons of Israel be like the sand of the sea, it is the remnant that will be saved; ²⁸for the Lord will execute His word on the earth, thoroughly and quickly." ²⁹And just as Isaiah foretold, "Unless the Lord of Sabaoth had left to us a posterity, We would have become like Sodom, and would have resembled Gomorrah."

Summary The prophetic Scriptures support the proposition that God has chosen Gentiles, and rejected the majority of Jews.

Structural Layout

Hosea
  "call Not My people...my people"   Hosea 2:23
  "Called sons of living God"   Hosea 1:10
Isaiah
  "Though as sand of sea...only remnant saved"   Isaiah 10:22
  "Except left a seed...be like Sodom"   Isaiah 1:9

9:25-29 Commentary

Paul concludes the argument begun at Rom. 9:6 with a series of Old Testament quotations designed to provide scriptural support for his conclusions. The first set of quotations is from Hosea and is given to support the conclusion that Gentiles are included in God's election (Rom. 9:25-26). Both Hosea 1:10 and 2:23 were originally intended to refer to scattered Israel. How can Paul use them to refer to the Gentiles? It seems best to understand that Paul is applying the principle to the Gentiles in a typical fashion. In Hosea's time, the Gentiles mocked the scattered the people of God, declaring that they were not God's people. But God declared that He would deliver and vindicate them. So, in Paul's day, the Jews derided the Gentiles, declaring that they were not part of God's people. But God has also vindicated them and declares that they too are part of the people of God.

The second set of quotations is from Isaiah and is given to support the conclusion that only some of the physical descendants are part of God's elect nation (Rom. 9:27-29). The key words are *remnant* and *posterity*. A *remnant (hupoleimma)* is a small remaining portion of something that was much larger. The word translated *posterity* is the Greek word, *sperma*, seed. Both refer to a small portion in comparison to a larger group. Though the physical descendants are large in number, *as the sand of the sea*, yet the actual number elect is very small, a *remnant, a seed.*

Israel's Rejection was the Result of Their Disbelief 9:30-10:21

Summary Israel failed to attain righteousness because they would not accept the gospel message by faith; for they were determined to gain righteousness by their own self-effort.

Structural Layout

Israel did not arrive at law of righteousness
They did not submit to the righteousness of God
Christ is the end of Law for righteousness
Righteousness based on faith speaks...believe, confess
A disobedient and obstinate people

Overview

Having established the fact that God has rejected the majority of the Jews and that He can do so without being unfaithful in His promises to Israel, Paul now explains why the Jews have been rejected and Gentiles accepted. As such, Paul moves from a discussion of sovereign choice to a discussion of human responsibility.

The major thought is that Israel failed because they would not accept righteousness as a gift by faith (Rom. 9:31, Rom. 10:3, Rom. 10:16, Rom. 10:21). Instead they stubbornly kept trying to establish their own righteousness by works (Rom. 9:30-33).

Next, Paul states that their failure came because they failed to see that the Messiah inaugurated a new and different approach to gaining righteousness, an approach that demanded the abandonment of their attempts to gain righteousness by Law (Rom. 10:1-4).

This new approach is not based on works of the Law but rather is based exclusively on faith (Rom. 10:5-13). One must not attempt to duplicate the work of God, but instead accept His offer of salvation by faith.

Paul ends the section by demonstrating that Israel has no excuse for their failure (Rom. 10:14-21). They had every opportunity to believe; yet they stubbornly resisted God's appeals.

Israel's Rejection Summarized: They Failed to Believe 9:30-33

³⁰What shall we say then? That Gentiles, who did not pursue righteousness, attained righteousness, even the righteousness which is by faith; ³¹but Israel, pursuing a law of righteousness, did not arrive at that law.

³²Why? Because they did not pursue it by faith, but as though it were by works. They stumbled over the stumbling stone, ³³just as it is written, "Behold, I lay in Zion a stone of stumbling and a rock of offense, And he who believes in Him will not be disappointed."

Summary   Israel did not attain righteousness because they sought it by works, but the Gentiles, who did not seek it, attained it by faith.

Structural Layout

Gentiles	Israel
did not pursue righteousness	pursued law of righteousness
attained righteousness	did not arrive at that law
by faith	not by faith, but by works
	stumbled over stumbling stone

9:30-33 Commentary

This section introduces the reason for Israel's rejection and in contrast states the reason for the Gentiles acceptance. First, Paul states that the Gentiles succeeded in gaining righteousness but Israel did not (Rom. 9:30-31). Then, Paul explains why Israel failed (Rom. 9:32-33).

9:30-31. Paul asks, *What shall we say then?* That is, what can be summarized from the discussion of the vessels of mercy and vessels of wrath in the last section? First, *that Gentiles attained righteousness.* These Gentiles were not even trying to gain righteousness. *They did not pursue it.* Yet, they attained it on the basis of faith. Yet, *Israel, pursuing a law of righteousness, did not arrive at that law.* They were attempting to gain righteousness by mean of law and they failed to gain it. Paul makes it clear that the problem was not related to zeal or personal effort since the Gentiles put forth no effort, while Israel was making serious effort.

9:32-33. So, *why* then did Israel fail? Israel's problem was in their method, not in their effort. They were attempting to gain righteousness *by works*, rather than *by faith.* As a result, they *stumbled over the stumbling stone.* Israel rejected their own Messiah (Jn. 1:11). Paul combines two passages, Isa 8:14 and Isa 28:16. Christ is the stone (Luke 20:17-18; 1 Pet. 2:4-8). Yet, this stone elicits two very different responses. To those who come to Him by faith, He is the precious cornerstone (Ps. 118:22), but to those who approach Him in their own self-righteousness, He is a *stone of stumbling and rock of offense.*

Israel's Zeal Was Pointed in the Wrong Direction   10:1-4

[1]Brethren, my heart's desire and my prayer to God for them is for their salvation. [2]For I testify about them that they have a zeal for God, but not in accordance with knowledge. [3]For not knowing about God's righteousness and seeking to establish their own, they did not subject themselves to the righteousness of God. [4]For Christ is the end of the law for righteousness to everyone who believes.

Summary   Israel's zeal was pointed in the wrong direction towards works and away from faith in Christ.

Structural Layout

> They have a zeal for God
>> not in accordance with knowledge

> not knowing about God's righteousness
> seeking to establish own righteousness
> They did not submit to righteousness of God
> Christ is end of the Law for righteousness
> for everyone who believes.

10:1-4 Commentary

In this section Paul states that Israel's failure came because they failed to see that the Messiah inaugurated a new and different approach to gaining righteousness, an approach that demanded the abandonment of their attempts to gain righteousness by Law.

10:1-2. Paul begins by expressing his concern for Israel. As in Rom. 9:1-3, he does so to eliminate any idea that his words are motivated by animosity towards his own people. Paul's concern is heightened when he considers Israel's *zeal for God.* In some ways Israel was fanatically religious. Yet this zeal was worthless because it employed a method for gaining righteousness that would not work. It was *not in accordance with knowledge.* They had a tragic misunderstanding of God's ways.

10:3. Paul explains that their failure is due to *not knowing about God's righteousness.* As in Rom. 1:17 and Rom. 3:22 this righteousness refers to the righteousness that God gives as a gift, not to his righteous character. Does this lack of knowledge excuse Israel? Not according to Rom. 10:19-20. This lack of knowledge about righteousness from God by faith is a self-imposed ignorance. Their zeal for the Law should have led them to realize that they would never gain righteousness by Law. Their study of the stories of their forefathers and of the writings of the prophets should have led them to an awareness that righteousness is gained by faith. However, it was their conceit-driven zeal for self-righteousness that blinded them from the truth. The parable in Luke 18:9-14 is a good example of this blindness.

10:4. Paul concludes the section by stating that Israel, when confronted by their Messiah, should have abandoned their attempts at gaining righteousness by Law and instead should have accepted righteousness by faith. The statement, *For Christ is the end of the law for righteousness to everyone who believes* has been understood in several different ways. Three suggestions have been offered for the meaning of the word, *end (telos)*. Some suggest that Christ is the fulfillment of the Law. However, *end* does not mean fulfillment. Others suggest that Christ is the goal of the Law. The word can mean goal but this idea does not fit as well in this context. It is best to see Christ as the termination of Law. Yet, this termination should not be thought of as a shift in the age, as though the age of Law has been replaced by the age of Grace. Rather, the idea is more personal. When confronted by the Messiah, one stops attempting to gain righteousness through the works of Law, but instead responds by faith to Messiah's offer of righteousness. This was just as true for the Old Testament saints as it is true today.

Faith Righteousness and Law Righteousness Contrasted   10:5-13

⁵For Moses writes that the man who practices the righteousness which is based on law shall live by that righteousness.

⁶But the righteousness based on faith speaks as follows: "Do not say in your heart, 'Who will ascend into heaven?' (that is, to bring Christ down), ⁷or 'Who will descend into the abyss?' (that is, to bring Christ up from the dead)."

⁸But what does it say? "The word is near you, in your mouth and in your heart"— that is, the word of faith which we are preaching, ⁹that if you confess with your mouth Jesus as Lord, and believe in your heart that God raised Him from the dead, you will be saved; ¹⁰for with the heart a person believes, resulting in righteousness, and with the mouth he confesses, resulting in salvation. ¹¹For the Scripture says, "Whoever believes in Him will not be disappointed." ¹²For there is no distinction between Jew and Greek; for the same Lord is Lord of all, abounding in riches for all who call on Him; ¹³for "Whoever will call on the name of the Lord will be saved."

Summary Faith righteousness does not attempt to duplicate the saving work of Christ, but rather accepts by faith the gospel message.

Structural Layout

> righteousness based on law
>> man who practices shall live
>
> but
>
> righteousness based on faith
> Does not say
>> Who will ascend to bring Christ down?
>> Who will descend to raise Christ up?
>
> Does say
>> The word of faith is near you
>> confess...believe
>> Whoever believes in Him
>> Whoever will call

10:5-13 Commentary

In this section Paul contrasts Israel's approach of gaining righteousness by self-effort under Law with God's approach of giving righteousness by faith.

10:5. Paul begins with an analysis of *the righteousness which is based on law*. The difference between this righteousness and the righteousness based on faith (Rom. 10:6) is that of source and methodology for attaining it. This type of righteousness is attained only through performance of the Law. It is *the man who practices* the law who *shall live* by it (Lev 18:5). In Leviticus 18:1-5 the Lord appeals to Israel not to do what the Egyptians and the Canaanites do but instead to do His statues and judgments. Only by doing the Law will an individual *live*. Paul reiterates this idea, that law righteousness requires persistent works, in Rom. 2:13 and Gal 3:12. The Law is a system of doing. He also previously asserted that the Law did contain the promise of life for those who could meet its requirement (Rom. 7:10). If there would ever be a person who perfectly did what the Law required, he would *live by that righteousness*.

10:6-13. In the remainder of the section Paul presents the alternative to the works orientation of Law righteousness. He personifies *the righteousness based on faith*. This is the righteousness that is from God by faith (Rom. 1:17, Rom. 3:22, Rom. 9:30).

A thorough understanding of Deuteronomy 30 is essential to the study of Romans 10:6-13. Paul alludes to Moses' words in Deuteronomy 30:11-14 where he challenges the people to obey the Law by internalizing that Law through a heart-relationship with God. This he says after promising them restoration following God's banishment of them from the land (Deut. 30:1-10). This banishment happened because they forsook His covenant and followed other gods (Deut. 29:26). Paul associates this heart-relationship with faith in the gospel.

10:6-7. Paul uses Deuteronomy 30:11-14 in two ways. First, he sees in the passage what the righteousness by faith is not (*do not say...*). Paul sees in the questions an allusion to the finished work of Christ starting with His incarnation, *to bring Christ down*, and ending with His resurrection, *to bring Christ up from the dead.* Those who come to God by faith for righteousness realize that it is impossible through human effort to duplicate the work of God in Christ. The only way that God, the Father, could offer us righteousness was to have His Son become a man and die for our sins and then to raise Him from the dead (Rom. 3:21-26). We cannot duplicate this work, and thus we can never perform the work that must be done to save ourselves.

10:8-10 In contrast, Paul sees in Deuteronomy 30:11-14 the idea that the gospel message, *the word of faith which we are preaching,* is available. *The word is near you, in your mouth and in your heart.* Those who seek righteousness from God realize that the only way of acquiring this righteousness is by faith in the gospel message. *It is the word of faith.* Paul expands this thought, using the words, *confess* and *believe.* Does confession imply a work? No. Faith is an inner dynamic that produces external responses. To view confession as a work would contradict Paul's thesis (Rom. 1:16-17, Rom. 3:21-22). Yet it is correct to infer that without the external response, we can question the presence of the internal dynamic (Jam. 2:14-26). Paul says that we must *confess Jesus as Lord.* What does Paul mean by lord? In Deut. 30, Lord refers to Yahweh. It was to Him that Israel must return with all their hearts (Deut. 30:2). So, it seems clear that Paul is applying this to Christ, whom he sees as

Yahweh. In addition, Moses tells the people that when they return, they must obey the Lord (Deut. 30:8) and observe His commandments (Deut. 30:12). It is clear that Moses saw no distinction between a heart response to God and a life of obedience. Along with being one's savior and God, he must also be one's master. To confess Christ as Lord is not simply to acknowledge the fact that He is God. Rather one acknowledges that He is God and as such merits the obedience of our lives. We are now His slaves (Rom. 6:18).

11-13. Paul ends the section by quoting Isa. 28:16 and Joel 2:32. Both passages emphasize the universal access to this salvation by faith. It is available to both Jews and Gentiles since God is the God of all and responds to the faith of all. He reiterates the common status of each group because of sin (Rom. 3:9-10) and the common lordship of Christ (Rom. 3:29).

Israel is Without Excuse for Failing to Believe   10:14-21

[14]How then will they call on Him in whom they have not believed? How will they believe in Him whom they have not heard? And how will they hear without a preacher? [15]How will they preach unless they are sent? Just as it is written, "How beautiful are the feet of those who bring good news of good things!" [16]However, they did not all heed the good news; for Isaiah says, "Lord, who has believed our report?" [17]So faith comes from hearing, and hearing by the word of Christ. [18]But I say, surely they have never heard, have they? Indeed they have; "Their voice has gone out into all the earth, And their words to the ends of the world." [19]But I say, surely Israel did not know, did they? First Moses says, "I will make you jealous by that which is not a nation, By a nation without understanding will I anger you." [20]And Isaiah is very bold and says, "I was found by those who did not seek Me, I became manifest to those who did not ask for Me." [21]But as for Israel He says, "All the day long I have stretched out My hands to a disobedient and obstinate people."

Summary Israel has no excuse for their unbelief; for the message was clearly presented to them yet they stubbornly refused to accept it.

Structural Layout

> Send → preach → hear → believe →call
>> So faith comes by hearing
> They did not heed
>
> Surely they never heard, have they?
>> They have... "Their voice has gone out"
> Surely Israel did not know, did they?
>> "I was found by those who sought me not"
>
> But Israel   "a disobedient and obstinate people"

10:14-21 Commentary

Paul concludes chapter ten by showing that Israel had no excuse for their failure to believe. He begins by outlining the process that leads to salvation (Rom. 10:14-17). Then Paul demonstrates that the step in the process where the failure occurred was in Israel's failure to believe (Rom. 10:18-21).

10:14-17. Paul employs a series of rhetorical questions to outline the process that leads to salvation. The process includes sending, preaching, hearing, believing, and calling. Paul confirms the steps in the process by quoting Isa 52:7, *How beautiful are the feet of those who bring good news of good things!* At the same time, the quotation seems to hint at Paul's claim that the problem was not in sending, preaching, or hearing. The gospel has been preached. Yet, Paul admits that there was a breakdown somewhere in the process. For *Isaiah says, "Lord, who has believed our report?"* (Isa 53:1). Some did not believe. Again, there is a clear hint that the breakdown was not in sending, preaching, or hearing. The Lord had sent Isaiah and he had preached. The failure did not occur within the first three steps.

Before turning to a discussion of where the failure did occur, Paul summarizes the process and emphasizes that the object of faith is Christ. *So, faith comes from hearing, and hearing by the word of Christ.* Paul sees faith as the last step in the process of salvation. He understands that faith is impossible without God graciously providing the gospel message and proclaiming it through preachers. However, Paul does not suggest that God gives faith directly as a gift. It is the responsibility of the individual to respond to God's offer. This response will either be that of belief or unbelief. Faith must be in the gospel, *the word of Christ*. It is not the word which Christ spoke but the message about Christ. Christ is the object of this message (Rom. 1:3).

10:18-21. Paul next raises two questions suggesting that Israel has an excuse for their failure to believe. The first question, *surely they have never heard, have they*, suggests they never heard the message. Paul rejects this idea and quotes Psalm 19:4 to prove that they have heard. The Psalm speaks of natural revelation, the heavenly bodies (Ps 19:1). The revelation of God in nature is just as sufficient to condemn the Jews, as it was to condemn the Gentiles (Rom. 1:19-20). Beyond natural revelation, the Jews also had the prophetic message (Rom. 10:6). Their failure to respond cannot be blamed on their failure to hear the message.

A second question, *surely Israel did not know, did they*, raises the possibility that the message, though given, was too difficult for Israel to understand. This seems to be the best way to understand the word, *know*. Paul offers two quotations to demonstrate that the problem was not that the message was difficult to understand. The first passage, Deut. 32:21, describes the Gentiles as a people without much intelligence with reference to spiritual things. Yet Gentiles were able to understand the message and to respond to it by faith. The second passage, Isa. 65:1, describes the Gentiles as a people without much motivation to learn. Yet they learned from the message and responded in faith. If the message was so easily understood by those without much spiritual intelligence or motivation, it most certainly could have been understood by Israel.

Finally, Paul quotes from Isa. 65:2 to demonstrate that the problem was in the heart of those who heard. *All the day long I have stretched out My hands to a disobedient and obstinate people.* In spite of God's constant appeals to them (*stretching out His hands*), they stubbornly refused to believe. Clearly, they are without excuse for their failure to believe.

Israel's Rejection is Partial and Temporary 11:1-36

Summary   There is currently a gracious remnant of Jews being saved and in the future, there will be a national revival that will lead to national salvation.

Structural Layout

> God rejected His people?   Never!
>   There has come to be a remnant according to God's gracious choice.
> They did not stumble so as to fall? Never!
>   All Israel will be saved.

Overview

The structure of the chapter is marked by two rhetorical questions found in Rom. 11:1 and Rom. 11:11. They indicate the basic topic of discussion for the whole chapter, namely the nature of God's rejection of Israel. Does the fact that Israel is without excuse for their failure to gain righteousness by faith imply that God has finally and completely rejected Israel? Such a conclusion would contradict His eternal choice of Israel (Deut. 4:37). Paul takes up the question in chapter eleven.

He begins by showing that the current rejection of Israel is only partial (Rom. 11:1-10). As it was in the days of Elijah, so it is now. *In the same way then, there has also come to be at the present time a remnant according to God's gracious choice* (Rom. 11:5). He then demonstrates that the current rejection will be replaced by national salvation (Rom. 11:11-32). *And so, all Israel will be saved* (Rom. 11:26). This leads Paul to praise God for His wisdom in His dealings (Rom. 11:33-36).

Israel's Rejection is Partial 11:1-10

¹I say then, God has not rejected His people, has He? May it never be! For I too am an Israelite, a descendant of Abraham, of the tribe of Benjamin. ²God has not rejected His people whom He foreknew. Or do you not know what the Scripture says in the passage about Elijah, how he pleads with God against Israel? ³"Lord, they have killed Your prophets, they have torn down Your altars, and I alone am left, and they are seeking my life." ⁴But what is the divine response to him? "I have kept for Myself seven thousand men who have not bowed the knee to Baal." ⁵In the same way then, there has also come to be at the present time a remnant according to God's gracious choice. ⁶But if it is by grace, it is no longer on the basis of works, otherwise grace is no longer grace.

⁷What then? What Israel is seeking, it has not obtained, but those who were chosen obtained it, and the rest were hardened; ⁸just as it is written, "God gave them a spirit of stupor, Eyes to see not and ears to hear not, Down to this very day." ⁹And David says, "Let their table become a snare and a trap, And a stumbling block and a retribution to them. ¹⁰"Let their eyes be darkened to see not, And bend their backs forever."

Summary Israel's current rejection is only partial; for God has chosen a gracious remnant of believing Jews just as He did in the days of Elijah.

Structural Layout

> God rejected His people?   Never!
>> whom He foreknew
> I am Israelite
> Elijah
>> pleaded against Israel
>> I have kept 7000
> In same way
>> remnant according to God's gracious choice
>> those chosen obtained

11:1-10 Commentary

In Rom. 9:30-10:21, Paul has shown that Israel failed to gain righteousness due to their stubborn refusal to abandon self-righteousness and believe the gospel. Their failure has led to divine rejection. Does this rejection mean an end to God's dealings with Israel?

In his typical style Paul introduces this potential implication with a rhetorical question which he immediately rejects (Rom. 11:1a). This is followed by his explanation (Rom. 11:1b-6) which in turn is followed by a summary conclusion concerning Israel's situation (Rom. 11:7-10).

11:1a. *God has not rejected his people, has He?* That those who did not believe are rejected is certainly the case. The question seems to refer to a complete and absolute rejection. Paul references Israel in several different ways. Israel sometimes refers to the elect nation, sometimes to the believing remnant, and sometimes to those who have rejected Christ. To properly understand Paul's statements, one must properly identify the Israel about which he talks. In this instance, *His people* must refer to the elect nation. That is, the nation to which God gave national promises. So, the question he is asking is whether God has abandoned His program for Israel as an elect nation. Paul rejects this conclusion, *May it never be!* Such a conclusion would tarnish God's name (1 Sam. 12:22). Though God would discipline His people, His covenant with them is as sure as the laws of the universe (Jer. 33:25-26).

11:1b-2a. Paul begins his explanation by using himself as an example of a Jew whom God has not rejected. He *too is an Israelite, a descendant of Abraham, of the tribe of Benjamin.* Paul includes himself as part of spiritual Israel (Rom. 9:6). This leads him to affirm positively the truth of Israel's election and God's continued commitment to the nation. *God has not rejected His people whom He foreknew.* The term, *foreknew,* is only used in conjunction with divine choice and so must indicate that Israel, as a nation is elect (Rom. 8:29, 1 Pet 1:2, Acts 2:23). This certainly is confirmed throughout the Old Testament (Deut. 7:6, Ps. 33:12, Isa. 45:4). The concept of divine choice is woven throughout Rom. 11:4-6.

11:2b-4. Next, Paul compares the present situation to the days of Elijah when it seemed that apostasy had completely overtaken Israel. Under the influence of Jezebel, the foreign wife of Ahab, king of Israel, Israel had fallen deeply into Baal worship (1 Kg. 17-18). This led to a conflict between Elijah and the prophets of Baal on Mount Carmel (1 Kg. 18:20-40). The conflict ended with a great victory for the Lord and the slaying of 850 prophets of Baal and Asherah who were supported by Jezebel. In response Jezebel swore to Elijah that she would kill him (1 Kg 19:1-2). Elijah fled in fear to the wilderness where in depression was ready to give up (1 Kg 19:3-4). There he spoke to the Lord, explaining that the situation was hopeless. *They have killed Your* *prophets, they have torn down Your altars, and I alone am left, and they are seeking my life* (1 Kg 19:10). Paul understood the conversation as Elijah *pleadings with God against Israel.* However, God revealed to Elijah that *He had kept seven thousand who had not bowed the knee to Baal* (1 Kg. 19:18). This keeping was a matter of divine sovereignty and reflects the language of Rom. 9. Yet, the language does not suggest that God's election determined the responses of these individuals. It only suggests that God sovereignly protected them as part of His eternal plan.

11:5-6. Paul next compares God's response to Elijah with the current situation. There is currently a *remnant according to God's gracious choice.* Paul is picking up on the *remnant* language found in Rom. 9:27-29 and on sovereignty language of his preceding statement from God. In Rom. 9 Israel was described as a remnant in a negative sense to demonstrate that only a few of the physical descendants of Israel are part of spiritual Israel. Now he sees a more positive idea in the term. The remnant also suggests that God is not finished with Israel. Though it is small, there remains a remnant. This remnant is *according to God's gracious choice.* This statement is again designed to correct the Jewish concept of God's elective choice. It is not a choice based on physical descent or on works. It is *by grace.* It is not *on the basis of works,* for then God would be required to choose those who succeed (Rom. 4:4) and reject those who fail. Either God's choice is a matter of unmerited grace, or it is a matter of merited reward. The two are mutually exclusive. *Otherwise grace is no longer grace.*

11:7-10. Paul concludes that *what Israel is seeking, it has not obtained.* In this instance, Israel refers to the nation as a whole. The majority of the Jews is in disbelief and has thus failed to gain righteousness by means of works (Rom. 9:31). But, God chose some who obtained righteousness by faith. *The rest were hardened.* As in Rom. 9:18, the hardening is best understood as the response of God to human rejection of Him. Paul confirms this by quoting Isa. 29:10 and Deut. 29:4 and then Ps. 69:22-23. In Isa. 29 the Lord is pronouncing his judgment upon Ariel (Jerusalem) because of their sin. God responds by sending the nations to wage war against Jerusalem. All this will

141

leave the inhabitants with *a spirit of stupor*. The addition of Deut. 29:4 is given by Paul to suggest that this rejection of the Lord has continued down to the present day. But does Deut. 29:4 suggest that the reason for their failure to believe was due to God's sovereign choice? Did He choose not to give them *a heart to know, nor eyes to see, nor ears to hear* (Deut. 29:4)? This does not seem to be Moses' intent. Rather he is reproving their dullness in the past. Thus, the hardening is a response in the form of divine judgment because of their rejection of God. Ps. 69:22-23 is an imprecation upon David's enemies because of their opposition to him. Again, the hardening is a matter of response in the form of divine judgment. So it is with the majority of Jews. They have rejected their Messiah and as a result are under God's hardening.

Israel's Rejection is Temporary   *11:11-32*

¹¹I say then, they did not stumble so as to fall, did they? May it never be!

But by their transgression salvation has come to the Gentiles, to make them jealous. ¹²Now if their transgression is riches for the world and their failure is riches for the Gentiles, how much more will their fulfillment be! ¹³But I am speaking to you who are Gentiles. Inasmuch then as I am an apostle of Gentiles, I magnify my ministry, ¹⁴if somehow I might move to jealousy my fellow countrymen and save some of them. ¹⁵For if their rejection is the reconciliation of the world, what will their acceptance be but life from the dead?

¹⁶If the first piece of dough is holy, the lump is also; and if the root is holy, the branches are too. ¹⁷But if some of the branches were broken off, and you, being a wild olive, were grafted in among them and became partaker with them of the rich root of the olive tree, ¹⁸do not be arrogant toward the branches; but if you are arrogant, remember that it is not you who supports the root, but the root supports you. ¹⁹You will say then, "Branches were broken off so that I might be grafted in." ²⁰Quite right, they were broken off for their unbelief, but you stand by your faith. Do not be conceited, but fear; ²¹for if God did not spare the natural branches, He will not spare you, either. ²²Behold then the kindness and severity of God; to those who fell, severity, but to you, God's kindness, if you continue in His kindness; otherwise you also will be cut off. ²³And they also, if they do not continue in their unbelief, will be grafted in, for God is able to graft them in again. ²⁴For if you were cut off from what is by nature a wild olive tree, and were grafted contrary to nature into a cultivated olive tree, how much more will these who are the natural branches be grafted into their own olive tree?

²⁵For I do not want you, brethren, to be uninformed of this mystery—so that you will not be wise in your own estimation—that a partial hardening has happened to Israel until the fullness of the Gentiles has come in; ²⁶and so all Israel will be saved; just as it is written, "The Deliverer will come from Zion, He will remove ungodliness from Jacob." ²⁷"This is My covenant with them, When I take away their sins." ²⁸from the standpoint of the gospel they are enemies for your sake, but from the standpoint of God's choice they are beloved for the sake of the fathers; ²⁹for the gifts and the calling of God are irrevocable. ³⁰For just as you once were disobedient to God, but now have been shown mercy because of their disobedience, ³¹so these also now have been disobedient, that because of the mercy shown to you they also may now be shown mercy. ³²For God has shut up all in disobedience so that He may show mercy to all.

Summary   Israel's current rejection is only temporary; for God's program of Gentile salvation is purposed to draw them back, a purpose confirmed by revelation.

Structural Layout

> They did not stumble so as to fall?   Never!
>> Salvation has come to Gentiles to make them jealous
>>> If they do not continue in unbelief,
>> God will graft them in
>> God is able
>
>> This mystery
>> A partial hardening to Israel
>>> until the fullness of the Gentiles
>> Thus all Israel will be saved.

11:11-32 Commentary

Again, Paul introduces a new aspect of the discussion with a rhetorical question; *they did not stumble so as to fall, did they?* (Rom. 11:11a). The question asks if Israel's current rejection of their Messiah, the act of stumbling (Rom. 9:32-33) is a permanent falling. Paul rejects this idea in his normal fashion and then takes the rest of the section (Rom. 11:11b-32) to explain why this is not the case.

He argues first that the current program of Gentile salvation is purposed to entice Israel back (Rom. 11:11b-15). He then uses the illustration of grafting branches on trees to suggest that God is able to restore Israel (Rom. 11:16-24). He also uses this as an occasion to warn the Gentiles about arrogance toward Israel. Finally, he reveals that prophetic revelation predicts Israel's restoration (Rom. 11:25-32).

11:11a. With the question, *they did not stumble so as to fall, did they*, Paul introduces the second aspect of God's rejection, namely that it is temporary. *They* must be understood as referring to the elect nation as a whole since the question parallels the question made in Rom. 11:1. The distinction between stumbling and falling is the distinction between what is permanent and what is temporary. When one stumbles, one is shaken and loses balance. But not everyone who stumbles actually falls. The proposition is that Israel as a nation has stumbled in unbelief but has not fallen into irrecoverable rejection by God.

11:12-15. Paul provides the first of three arguments in support of this proposition. Paul argues that God's current program of Gentile salvation is purposed to woo them back. This is seen in the phrase, *to make them jealous*. That this jealousy is associated with salvation is seen in Rom. 11:14 in the expression, *to move to jealousy and save some*. The idea is to motivate the Jews to want salvation by seeing Gentiles gaining it.

It was with this goal in mind that Paul promoted his ministry as an *apostle of Gentiles* (Rom. 11:13-14). He let it be known that God had sent him to the Gentiles (Acts 22:21). He wanted to *move to jealousy his fellow countrymen and save some of them*. In this respect, Paul used his ministry to the Gentiles to evangelize the Jews.

Paul also argues that this will result in benefit for the Gentiles who have believed. He argues from the lesser to the greater (Rom. 11:12, Rom. 11:15). The two verses parallel each other. As a result of *their transgression* and *their rejection* God has provided *riches* and *reconciliation* to the world. God is now offering salvation to the Gentiles. What can we expect when their *fulfillment* and *acceptance* occurs? Paul predicts a time when Israel will as a whole accept their Messiah. There will be a national revival. This will result in *much more* even for the Gentiles. It will result in *life from the dead*. This will be the time of physical resurrection and heavenly bliss.

The expression, *their fulfillment*, in Rom. 11:12 is best translated, fullness. This is the same term used in Rom. 11:25. It refers to a time of national restoration for Israel during which there will be national revival and salvation. This returning to faith will end their rejection and inaugurate a time of divine acceptance (Rom. 11:15), the millennial kingdom.

11:16-24. Paul gives a second argument supporting the idea that God's rejection of Israel is temporary. It also includes a warning to the Gentiles against arrogance.

The argument, begun with an illustration of *dough*, shifts to an illustration of an *olive tree* (Rom. 11:16). The two illustrations are parallel. The *root* of the olive tree refers to the patriarchs, especially Abraham. They were the *firstfruits* of Israel. The root is *holy* in the sense that it is set apart to God, consecrated to Him and recipient of His covenanted promises. The *branches* refer to the natural descendants, the Jews. They too are recipients of the promises as long as they are attached to the root.

Two actions now take place (Rom. 11:17). First, the natural branches are *broken off*. This represents the rejection of individual Jews by God because of their unbelief. Second, *wild olive branches were grafted in*. This represents the acceptance of individual Gentiles by God because of their belief.

This leads Paul parenthetically to warn the Gentiles against *arrogance* (Rom. 11:18-22). The Gentile is addressed directly using a singular, *you*, in the same way that Paul had addressed the Jews in Rom. 2. Gentile arrogance against Jews is just as serious as Jewish arrogance against Gentiles and warrants the same kind of response. Gentile arrogance would arise from the idea that God's replacement of Jews with Gentiles in Rom. 11:17 was based on some merit that He saw in them. They would conclude, *branches were broken off so that I might be grafted in*. This was not the case. Paul's response, *quite right*, is not an agreement with their conclusion. It rather introduces a correction.

The Gentile is right that the branches were broken off but not right as to the reason. The only reason the Jews were rejected was because of *their unbelief* and the only reason Gentiles were accepted was because *of their faith*. In faith there is no room for boasting and arrogance (Rom. 3:27).

Thus, the Gentiles should not be *conceited but fear*. *If God did not spare the natural branches, He will not spare you, either*. Does this conditional statement imply that one can lose salvation? No. The cutting off of Jews in Rom. 11:17 did not mean the loss of salvation, but the loss of what was potentially theirs. So too, salvation has been offered to the Gentiles. When Gentiles fail to believe, they too are cut off from the potential that is theirs in the gospel.

Finally, Paul uses the illustration to show that Israel's return is possible (Rom. 11:23-24). He argues that God, who has already done the more difficult task of *grafting* in the Gentiles, *the wild branches*, can certainly *graft* in the Jews, *the natural branches*. This is an argument from the greater to the lesser. God has already done the greater. *Much more* He is capable of doing the lesser. *God is able to graft them in again*. The only thing that is necessary is faith on the part of Jews.

11:25-32. Paul offers a third argument supporting the idea that God's rejection of Israel is temporary. Then Paul ends with some final words about Israel and their position with God.

Paul writes about a *mystery* in Rom. 11:25. Paul refers to a revelation from God which in the past has been kept secret (Rom. 16:25-26). In this instance, the secret is that Israel's rejection is partial (Rom. 11:25) and that Israel will one day be restored (Rom. 11:26).

Paul begins by stating that the current partial *hardening of Israel* will continue *until the fullness of the Gentiles has come in*. Paul uses fullness as he did in Rom. 11:12. It refers to that time when all the Gentiles chosen by God will have gained salvation. This point becomes the point at which the hardening of Israel comes to an end. At this point, *all Israel will be saved*. *All Israel* has been interpreted in two very different ways. Amillennialist see it referring to the elect of all ages, to a spiritual Israel composed of Jews and Gentiles. Thus, all Israel is the Church. They claim that this is Paul's intention in Rom. 9:6 also. They argue that *so (houtōs)* suggests a logical conclusion rather than a chronological conclusion. However, there is good reason to interpret the phrase as referring to a future national regathering of Israel. First, the term, *Israel,* throughout the chapter refers to the physical nation, not to the general elect. Second, the use of *until* in Rom. 11:25 establishes a chronological relationship. Third, the quotation that follows refers specifically to the nation of Israel, not to the elect in general. Fourth, the idea of a national regathering is also described with the terms, *acceptance* (Rom. 11:15) and *fullness* (Rom. 11:12).

The time sequence is as follows. Currently God is working primarily with Gentiles in the church and Israel as a nation is hardened. In the future, God will complete his work among Gentiles (Rom. 11:25). At that time, God will renew His plans for Israel (Rom. 11:26a). Christ will return and set up His millennial kingdom (Rom. 11:26b-27). Paul confirms this by quoting from Isa 59:20-21; *"The Deliverer will come from Zion, He will remove ungodliness from Jacob. This is My covenant with them, when I take away their sins."* Paul stresses that the time of this revival will be when Jesus returns. The revival will be the time when the Lord fulfills His covenant promises to Israel.

Paul concludes the section (Rom. 11:28-29) by summarizing Israel's relationship with God. Individually *they are enemies* because they have not believed the *gospel.* However, in terms of national election *they are beloved for the sake of the fathers.* God made national promises to the patriarchs which He will fulfill. Such promises are *irrevocable.*

Paul ends by showing the similarities between God's dealings with the Gentiles and God's dealings with the Jews (Rom. 11:30-32). Both groups have been *disobedient.* To both groups God desires to be *merciful.* Paul's final statement, *For God has shut up all in disobedience so that He may show mercy to all,* sweeps back to the beginning of chapter one and thus suggests that Paul is drawing the logical segment of the epistle to a close. Both are disobedient (Rom. 1:18-3:20) and both have been shown mercy in the work of Christ (Rom. 3:31-4:25).

Final Words of Praise   *11:33-36*

³³*Oh, the depth of the riches both of the wisdom and knowledge of God! How unsearchable are His judgments and unfathomable His ways!* ³⁴*For who has known the mind of the Lord, or who became His counselor?* ³⁵*Or who has first given to Him that it might be paid back to him again?* ³⁶*For from Him and through Him and to Him are all things. To Him be the glory forever. Amen.*

Summary   **Praise God for His great wisdom and knowledge.**

Structural Layout

>   Oh, the depth of the riches of wisdom and knowledge of God!
>   How unsearchable, unfathomable
>   Who has known?
>   Who became His counselor?
>   Who first has given to Him?
>   from Him, Through Him, To Him are all things.
>   To Him be the glory forever.

11:33-36 Commentary

Contemplation about the greatness of God's mercy and wisdom in planning for both Jews and Gentiles moves Paul to a final doxology of praise. God alone was wise enough to create such a wonderful plan for the salvation of all. He alone is worthy of our praise.

How befitting that Paul ends his treatise on justification with praise and adoration to God. Truly *from Him and through Him and to Him are all things. To Him be the glory forever. Amen.*

Applying Justification in Christian Community   *12:1-15:13*

Summary   Christians must respond to God's mercies through sacrificial living, loving the brethren, submission to government, holy in actions, and unity with each other.

Structural Layout

> Present your bodies a living sacrifice
> Do not to think more highly of himself
> Let love be without hypocrisy
> Be in subjection to the governing authorities
> Love one another
> Put on Christ
> Accept one another without passing judgment

Overview

At Rom. 12:1 Paul begins the second major section of the book. This section is mainly applicational, filled with verbs in the imperative mood and appeals. Only four times did Paul use the imperative in Rom. 1:16-11:36 and all those occurred in Rom. 6. Twenty-nine imperatives occur in Rom. 12:1-15:13 and additionally Paul uses other forms that introduce appeals and exhortations such as *I urge, parakalō* (Rom. 12:1); *I say, legō* (Rom. 12:3); and *let us ...*, hortatory subjunctives (Rom. 14:13, 19). This pattern of dividing a letter into a doctrinal section and an applicational section is a common Pauline trait. He does so in Galatians, Ephesians, and Colossians.

The topics of his exhortations are generally agreed upon by expositors. They are as follows:

- General Foundational Exhortation   12:1-2
- Conceit over Spiritual Gifts   12:3-8
- Christian Love   12:9-21
- Submission to Government   13:1-7
- Loving Your Neighbor   13:8-10
- Holy Living in Light of Christ's Return   13:11-14

149

- Resolving Christian Disagreements   14:1-15:13

The major exhortation in Rom. 14:1-15:13 is clearly related to the issue of Jew/Gentile relationships. Romans 1:16-11:36 addressed the doctrinal issue and in Rom. 14:1-15:13 Paul addresses the social and cultural corollary. Jews and Gentile Christians at Rome were divided. The doctrinal issue led to socio-religious disputes that may have endangered Christian love and unity. The one issue that does not seem to be internal to the church was the issue of government found in chapter thirteen. It is unlikely that Paul would have addressed the issue if the Romans were not having some trouble in this area. Overall then, the instructions emphasize human relationships: unity, peace, and love both within the church and outside of it.

Foundational Exhortation: Dedicate Your Life to God   12:1-2

[1]Therefore I urge you, brethren, by the mercies of God, to present your bodies a living and holy sacrifice, acceptable to God, which is your spiritual service of worship. [2]And do not be conformed to this world, but be transformed by the renewing of your mind, so that you may prove what the will of God is, that which is good and acceptable and perfect.

Summary   Offer up yourselves to God as living sacrifices, not being molded to the world, but constantly being transformed from within.

Structural Layout

    I urge you
            by mercies of God
        to present your bodies a living sacrifice
        stop being conformed to this world
        be transformed
            by renewing of mind
            that you may prove the will of God: good, acceptable, perfect

12:1-2 Commentary

This first exhortation is foundational to all the exhortations that follow. It is an appeal for a broad commitment from the Christian out of which all the specific actions that follow flow. The connective, *therefore*, suggests that this commitment is the logical response to God's provision of salvation discussed in chapters 1-11.

12:1. Paul introduces the exhortation with the word, *urge, (parakaleō)*. The word means to beg, implore, or appeal. By this he appeals to the heart for a response. He does not appeal to fear or retribution. He does not command. Paul realized that the greatest and most pleasing motivation for obedience to God is thankfulness for all that He has done. *The mercies of God*, His acts of mercy in saving us, should be the motivation that prompts us to live for Him.

The exhortation is *to present your bodies a living and holy sacrifice*. Paul used the same verb, *paristēmi* in Rom. 6:13 where the motif was that of presenting yourself to God as a slave (Rom. 6:16). Now the motif is that of worship. Here the worshiper is presenting an offering to God. This was the usual verb used for such presentations (Luke 2:22). We are to present ourselves in dedication to God. Yet, not as a dead sacrifice, but as *a living and holy sacrifice*. *Bodies* refer to the total person, not just to the physical body. As such we must be *holy*. Though the word has some moral overtones, it seems best to understand it as referring to that which is completely consecrated to God, given over to His service (Lev. 2:3).

Some suggest that this presentation is to be a one-time act since the Greek verb is in the aorist tense. However, Greek scholars agree that the aorist tense does not indicate a once-for-all action. See Appendix B for a discussion of the aorist tense. It is best to understand the action to involve something that is to be done completely as a single act. This commitment is not something we progress toward, but rather a single act of the will. If later we abandon that commitment, then we must act again to renew it.

This act is our *spiritual service of worship*. The noun translated *service of worship* is *latreia*, and refers to the external activities associated with worship as reflected in the Levitical system (Rom. 9:4, Heb. 9:1, 6, 9). For the Christian, this service of worship is internal and involves the consecration of one's whole being (Rom. 1:9, Phil. 3:3, Heb. 9:6). The word, *spiritual*, *logikos*, can mean either logical or spiritual. However, the meaning, *spiritual*, best fits with the imagery of the temple service. The Levitical offerings were too often only ritual. For the Christian, the offering of self is the height of spiritual worship and consecration.

12:2. Paul describes this commitment with two additional imperatives. The verb tenses change from the aorist tense, used in verse one to the present tense, a tense of progressive continuous action. Once the commitment to God is made, the Christian enters into a life-long process of spiritual development. This development is viewed negatively and positively. To *be conformed to this world*, is to allow the world to mold your life. It emphasizes external form. The verb, *syschēmatizō* is a causative verb with the lexical root from the noun, *schēma*, an outward form or shape. The world, *aiōn*, does not refer to the material world, but to the immaterial morals, values, and beliefs that typify the age. So, to *be conformed to this world* is to allow yourself to be shaped by the morals, values, and beliefs of the world. To be *transformed by the renewing of your mind* is quite different. This transformation or metamorphosis is not simply external conformity, but is a change from the inside out. It involves a complete renovation of the mind (Titus 3:5; Col. 3:10). Mind, *nous*, focuses on one's way of thinking. Yet, here it is not dealing with logical thinking but moral reasoning as was the case in Rom. 1:28. Proper moral actions are the result of proper moral reasoning. We must be careful not to simply conform to some external standard, even a good standard. The Christian life must be a transformation that begins on the inside and then surfaces in the activities of life.

Living as Members of the Church   *12:3-21*

Summary   We must exercise our gifts with humility and love the brethren without hypocrisy.

Structural Layout

> I say to every man not to think more highly of himself than he ought
> Let love be without hypocrisy
> Bless, rejoice, weep, be of the same mind, overcome evil with good.

Overview

The next two sections address Christians mainly as members of the Church. We are *one body* (Rom. 12:5). We are to be *devoted to one another* and *contributing to the needs of the saints* (Rom. 12:13). We are *to be of the same mind toward one another* (Rom. 12:16). On the other hand, Rom. 12:17-21 addresses our relationships with those outside of the church. These are the ones who attempt to *overcome you with evil* (Rom. 12:21). Paul speaks of our relationship with *all men* (Rom. 12:17-18). Yet, the paraenetic style of short commands seems to suggest that all these verses should be kept together.

The first exhortation (Rom. 12:3-8) deals with the humble exercise of spiritual gifts. This is followed by a series of commands that are related to Christian love (Rom. 12:9-13). Finally, Paul offers a paraenetic list of commands some dealing with internal church relationships and some dealing with external relationships (Rom. 3:14-21).

Exercise Spiritual Gifts with Humility   *12:3-8*

[3]For through the grace given to me I say to everyone among you not to think more highly of himself than he ought to think; but to think so as to have sound judgment, as God has allotted to each a measure of faith. [4]For just as we have many members in one body and all the members do not have the same function, [5]so we, who are many, are one body in Christ, and individually members one of another. [6]Since we have gifts that differ according to the grace given to us, each of us is to exercise them accordingly: if prophecy, according to the proportion of his faith; [7]if service, in his serving; or he who teaches, in his teaching; [8]or he who exhorts, in his exhortation; he who gives, with liberality; he who leads, with diligence; he who shows mercy, with cheerfulness.

Summary   Since we are all part of one body and we have differing abilities given by God, exercise your abilities humbly without conceit.

Structural Layout

> I say to every man
>> not to think more highly of himself than he ought
>> but to think with sound judgment
>>> as God has allotted to each
>>> we, who are many, are one body
>>> we have gifts that differ
>> let each exercise them accordingly:
>>>> prophecy, service, teaching,
>>>> exhorting, giving, leading, showing mercy
>>> according to proportion of faith
>>> with liberality
>>> with cheerfulness

12:3-8 Commentary

This exhortation (Rom. 12:3-8) deals with the humble exercise of spiritual gifts. The problem of conceit addressed by the exhortation seems to stem from the fact that individual members of the church had been given special abilities by God. Instead of using these gifts in humility, they became a source of conceit (Rom. 12:3). This may have been amplified by disunity within the church. Paul introduces his explanation with the connector, *for (gar)* at Rom. 12:4. Such conceit contradicts the nature and purposes of those gifts and the unity and interdependency characteristic of the church (Rom. 12:4-8).

12:3. The admonition, *not to think more highly of himself than he ought to think*, is a general exhortation against spiritual conceit. Paul has twice dealt with arrogance, first among Jews (Rom. 2:17-20) and then among the Gentiles (Rom. 11:20). In both cases he employed the singular, *you* in dramatic fashion. It seems that there was some spiritual conceit at Rome both with the Jewish Christians and the Gentile Christians. When this is coupled with giftedness, the natural tendency is to overestimate your value, to underestimate the value of others, and to assume that your abilities are self-produced. This is conceit, *thinking more highly than he ought*. Paul does not say that it is wrong to think highly of yourself. Christians ought to have a good self-image. We are created in the image of God. We are loved by God. We have been recreated into something valuable to God. We are trusted by God and have been given important responsibilities. We are gifted and useful.

However, we must not allow such thinking to lead to conceit. Thinking with *sound judgment* will keep us from this kind of conceit. Sound judgment involves a proper evaluation of who we are. Such thinking will lead to humility. First, we will recognize that our abilities come from God. *He has allotted to each a measure of faith.* This faith is not the faith expressed in salvation, but a faith necessary to exercise spiritual gifts (Rom. 12:6, Eph. 4:7-8). Our abilities are gifts given to us (Rom. 12:6). With each gift *allotted* to us by God, there is a parallel faith or confidence needed in the exercise of that gift. Both the gift and the confidence come from God.

12:4-5. Secondly, to think with sound judgment is to recognize that *we, who are many, are one body in Christ.* Being *many*, there is diversity and *all the members to not have the same function.* Yet, there is only *one body.* We recognize the unity and interdependency that we all have in the body of Christ. In the church, we complement each other. This should lead us to the humble conclusion that all are necessary and important. Paul develops this idea of the unity and diversity of the body in 1 Corinthians 12:12-27.

12:6-8. The proper response to this humble way of thinking is to be enthusiastically about the work that God has enabled you to do. So, Paul lists several *gifts* and the manners in which they should be exercised. Paul calls these gifts *charismata*, things that have been graciously bestowed or the results of grace, *charis* (1 Cor. 12:4). They are spiritual abilities bestowed upon the believer for speaking and serving in the church (1 Pet. 4:10-11). Like salvation, these gifts are neither earned nor deserved. They are gracious bestowments from God. The gifts differ *according to the grace given to us.* God graciously gives different gifts to different people (1 Cor. 12:8-10). These gifts are exercised *according to the proportion of his faith.* As in Rom. 12:3, faith refer to the confidence that is needed to exercise the gift. God gives the gifts but we must have confidence to exercise these new capabilities (1 Cor. 13:2).

The list of gifts (*prophecy, service, teaching, exhortation, giving,* and *showing mercy*) is representative, not exhaustive. Other lists are found in 1 Cor. 12:8-10, 1 Cor.

12:28, and Eph. 4:11. Three of the gifts fall under the category of speaking: prophecy, teaching, and exhortation. Though some understand prophecy as preaching, it is the revelatory aspect of the gift that distinguishes it from teaching and exhortation (1 Cor. 14:29-30). Teaching involves instruction. It is the ability to communicate God's truth to the minds of hearers. Exhortation involves encouraging and challenging listeners to respond. It is directed more to the will and heart. The additional four gifts fall under the category of service: serving, giving, leading, and showing mercy. Serving is a gift of helping others in the area of physical needs (1 Cor. 12:28, Acts 6:1). Giving is a special spirit of sharing personal resources with others. It was associated with those who had the means (Acts 4:34-35). Leading is the ability to govern or administer in the church (1 Cor. 12:28, 1 Tim. 5:17). Showing mercy involves performing acts of mercy for the needy (Matt. 9:27).

Paul's main purpose in listing the gifts is to motivate the readers to do what God had gifted them to do. Activity is a great way to overcome conceit and problems in interpersonal relationships. Paul adds several prepositional phrases to stress the zealous manner in which these gifts should be exercised. Do these things with *liberality*, *diligence*, and *cheerfulness*. Rather than allows spiritual gifts to become a source of inappropriate pride, we must zealously exercise our gifts in service to others.

Exercise Genuine Love in the Church   12:9-13

⁹Let love be without hypocrisy. Abhor what is evil; cling to what is good. ¹⁰Be devoted to one another in brotherly love; give preference to one another in honor; ¹¹not lagging behind in diligence, fervent in spirit, serving the Lord; ¹²rejoicing in hope, persevering in tribulation, devoted to prayer, ¹³contributing to the needs of the saints, practicing hospitality.

Summary Express genuine love in all of your relationships in the church.

156

Structural Layout

> Let love be without hypocrisy
>> Abhor what is evil, cling to what is good
>> Be devoted to one another in brotherly love
>> give preference to one another in honor
>> not lagging behind in diligence
>> fervent in spirit, serving the Lord
>> rejoicing in hope, persevering in tribulation, devoted to prayer
>> contributing to the needs of the saints, practicing hospitality

12:9-13 Commentary

The Greek structure makes it clear that sincere love is the topic of discussion. The words, *Love without hypocrisy*, form a title for what follows (Rom. 12:9a). The statement contains no verb but being part of a larger hortatory section, the word *let* or possibly *must be* fits well. The title is followed by a series of descriptive participle phrases most of which are translated as commands (Rom. 12:9b-13). These explain how genuine love expresses itself in various situations.

12:9a. *Let love be without hypocrisy* is the main exhortation in the section. This love is *agapē* love, a love of commitment and choice, covenantal love. It is to be *without hypocrisy, anupokritos,* genuine, not like an actor who simply masks his true feelings. The use of the term implies that hypocritical love does exist. Such love is a love that says but does not do the actions found in the rest of the section (James 2:15-16).

12:9b-13. The main exhortation in Greek is followed by a series of descriptive participles that explain how genuine love expresses itself in various situations. Though these are translated as additional independent commands, they are in fact modal participles that unpack how *agapē* love is applied in different situations. Paul begins with a set of two participles: *abhorring what is evil; clinging to what is good.* These form the two basic responses of genuine love. Love is moral in nature, exhibiting all the positive qualities that are associated with goodness and rejecting all the negative qualities that are associated with evil.

The Greek participle phrases found in Rom. 12:10-13 begin with a noun in the dative case followed by the participle. Our English translations tend to reverse the order, translating the dative with the preposition, *in*, assuming that the dative is a dative of means. However, these datives are more likely datives of reference, indicating the sphere or situation in which love is to be expressed. We might translate them as follows:

> With reference to brotherly love, *agape* love is devoted.
>
> With reference to honor, *agape* love gives preference to others.
>
> With reference to diligence, *agape* love does not lag behind
>
> With reference to spirit, *agape* love is fervent.
>
> With reference to the Lord, *agape* love serves.
>
> With reference to hope, *agape* love rejoices.
>
> With reference to tribulation, *agape* love perseveres.
>
> With reference to prayer, *agape* love is devoted.
>
> With reference to needy saints, *agape* love practices hospitality.

This translation reveals how pervasive love must be in all our relationships; and in many ways this description of *agape* love parallels Paul's beautiful description given in 1 Cor.13:4-8.

Exercise Goodness to Friends, Enemies and Neighbors   12:14-21

[14]*Bless those who persecute you; bless and do not curse.*

[15]*Rejoice with those who rejoice, and weep with those who weep.*

[16]*Be of the same mind toward one another; do not be haughty in mind, but associate with the lowly. Do not be wise in your own estimation.*

[17]*Never pay back evil for evil to anyone. Respect what is right in the sight of all men.* [18]*If possible, so far as it depends on you, be at peace with all men.* [19]*Never take your own revenge, beloved, but leave room for the wrath of God, for it is written, "Vengeance is Mine, I will repay," says the Lord.* [20]*"But if your enemy is hungry, feed him, and if he is thirsty, give him a drink; for in so doing you will heap burning coals on his head."* [21]*Do not be overcome by evil, but overcome evil with good.*

Summary Demonstrate goodness through blessing your enemies, empathizing with your friends, having no social prejudices, and avoiding acts of revenge.

> Bless those who curse you
> Rejoice with those who rejoice and weep with those who weep
> Be of same mind to one another
> Never pay back evil for evil

12:14-21 Commentary

The Greek structure of this section and the topics covered differ from Rom. 12:9-13 sufficiently to suggest a new section. Instead of a series of participles, Paul employs nine imperatives, that is direct commands (bless, do not curse, do not be, give, feed, give a drink, overcome) and two infinitives of command (rejoice, weep). However, it is possible to see this as a further description of our responsibility to love. If so, our responsibility to love is expanded beyond the church and includes both love of enemy and love of neighbor.

Paul uses imperative verbs in Rom. 12:14 and then infinitives in Rom. 12:15. Then in Rom. 12:16 Paul begins with participles and ties them to an imperative at the end of the verse. So, each verse seems to be a separate short paraenetic unit. The remaining section in Rom. 12:17-21 is a more developed exhortation marked off by the term, *evil* at the beginning and end.

12:14. *Bless those that persecute you.* When mistreated, we must express forgiveness and goodwill, not malice. The saying seems to be a direct quotation from the lips of Jesus (Luke 6:28) and expresses what it means to love your enemies (Luke 6:27).

12:15. To *Rejoice with those who rejoice, and weep with those who weep* is to express true empathy towards others (1 Cor.12:26). We must emotionally feel what others are feeling and enter into both their joys and sorrows.

12:16. To *be of the same mind toward one another* is to value all people in the same way. It is to have no social prejudices (James 2:1). If this is the case then you will *associate with the lowly*, those who are at the lowest social levels, the poor and the marginalized. The opposite is to *be haughty in mind* and to *be wise in* *your own estimation.* Social prejudices are direct violations of the command to love your neighbor (James 2:8-9).

12:17-21. Paul closes the section with a prohibition against personal retribution. Though in Greek the verbs in Rom. 12:17-19 are participles, the material seems to represent a new command. The word, *evil* marks the beginning and end of the section (Rom. 12:17, 21). Independent commands, that is imperative mood verbs in Greek, related to the main appeal are included (Rom. 12:19, 20, 21). The main appeal is to *never pay back evil for evil to anyone* (Rom. 12:17a). This appeal is then developed by a chain of commands given in a negative and positive manner with each elaborating on the main theme (Rom. 12:17b-20). Within the chain Paul offers Scripture to lend authority to his commands. The section concludes with a final summary command again expressed both negatively and positively (Rom. 12:21).

Never pay back evil for evil to anyone is the main command. Christians must never respond personally to evil with evil. Does this suggest that Christians should not participate in military or police activities? No! Paul is referring to taking personal revenge, taking the law into your own hands. It is clear from Rom. 13:4 that government does have the right to avenge evil. In our role as individuals we must not seek revenge. But when we function in roles within government, we have every right to inflict wrath as the appointed minister of God.

The opposite idea is first to *respect what is right in the sight of all men.* Paul refers to the general sense of right that exists in the world. Personal revenge is not our right. Even those who do evil have a right to be evaluated by government and either vindicated or condemned. When we seek personal revenge, we are denying the offender his or her rights. Second, we should *be at peace with all men.* Personal revenge leads to a never-ending cycle of war. Each act of evil leads to reciprocation with more evil. We must keep this cycle from beginning.

Paul reiterates the main command in a more specific way. *Never take your own revenge.* To pay back evil for evil is to seek revenge. Paul may have in mind Proverbs 20:22. The opposite is to *leave room for the wrath of God.* It is God's responsibility to punish evil doers. He has promised, *Vengeance is Mine, I will repay* (Deut. 32:35). When we take matters into our own hands, we are not trusting God to keep His word. How and when God takes vengeance Paul does not say. At times, He directly punishes evil doers during their lifetime. This is the idea of retribution theology, namely that God inflicts punishment through sickness, suffering, and other bad things upon those who evil; and that he blesses with good things those who are good. Though this is sometimes the case, we must be careful about drawing conclusions about a person's relationship with God based on the evil things that happen in their lives. This was Paul's point in chapter five and chapter eight. At other times God uses government as the agent of His wrath (Rom. 13:4). Still other times His wrath will be delayed until the final judgment (Heb. 10:29-30). One thing is certain, God's judgment upon evil will take place.

In contrast to taking vengeance, we should treat our enemies kindly. Paul quotes Proverbs 25:21-22. The idea of *heaping burning coals upon his head* must refer to something positive. I would make no sense to think that it refers to a back-door method to inflict punishment. Some have suggested that it speaks of producing repentance. Though a positive understanding that fits with our need to love even our enemies, it is hard to see how this figurative understanding can be drawn from the literal sense. It more likely refers to the custom of giving your neighbor coals for his fire. Fire was a very precious possession. The head was used to carry possessions from place to place. When you gave something to someone, they would carry it away on their heads. Thus, you should treat your enemy with great kindness, giving them food to eat, water to drink, and even coals for their fires.

The closing admonition, *do not be overcome by evil, but overcome evil with good*, summarizes the thought. We are not overcome by evil when evil people mistreat us or even kill us. We are overcome by evil when we respond to evil with evil. However, when we respond to evil with goodness, evil is conquered.

Living as Members of Society 13:1-14

Summary As members of society, submit to the authority of government, exercise love to your neighbor, and separate from a sinful world.

Structural Layout

> Let every person be in subjection to the governing authorities
> Owe nothing but to love one another
> Lay aside deeds of darkness and put on armor of light

Overview

The exhortations in chapter thirteen address our relationship to the state (Rom. 13:1-7); our love for our neighbors (Rom. 13:8-10); and our separation from the world in light of Christ's near return (Rom. 13:11-14). These deal mainly with our relationships within the broader society, though the exhortation to love one another does seem more directly related to our relationships within the church.

Submit to Civil Authorities 13:1-7

¹Every person is to be in subjection to the governing authorities.

For there is no authority except from God, and those which exist are established by God. ²Therefore whoever resists authority has opposed the ordinance of God; and they who have opposed will receive condemnation upon themselves.

³For rulers are not a cause of fear for good behavior, but for evil. Do you want to have no fear of authority? Do what is good and you will have praise from the same; ⁴for it is a minister of God to you for good. But if you do what is evil, be afraid; for it does not bear the sword for nothing; for it is a minister of God, an avenger who brings wrath on the one who practices evil.

⁵Therefore it is necessary to be in subjection, not only because of wrath, but also for conscience' sake.

⁶For because of this you also pay taxes, for rulers are servants of God, devoting themselves to this very thing. ⁷Render to all what is due them: tax to whom tax is due; custom to whom custom; fear to whom fear; honor to whom honor.

Summary   Submit to civil authorities since they are ordained by God for your good, and for the punishment of evil doers.

Structural Layout

Let every person be in subjection to the governing authorities
For
    those are established by God
    rules are:
        Minister of God to you for good
        Minister of God, avenger who brings wrath upon those who practice
evil
Wherefore
    be in subjection for wrath and for conscience sake.

13:1-7 Commentary

Paul begins with the command to submit to governing authorities (Rom. 13:1a). He offers two reasons why we should do so (Rom. 13:1b-5); then concludes with several concrete ways this submission should be applied (Rom. 13:6-7).

13:1a. Paul commands that Christians *be in subjection to the governing authorities.* Our position in Christ does not give us the right to ignore human authorities, even when those authorities are corrupt. The Roman government at the time when Paul wrote was often harsh, abusive, and cruel. Yet, Paul instructs the saints to submit. He reiterates this in Titus 3:1 as does Peter in 1 Pet 2:13. The verb expresses the idea of obedience.

13:1b-2. Paul offers two reasons why we should obey the government. First, we should obey because human government is *established by God* and thus derives its authority to rule from God (Rom. 13:1b). This is not to say that everything government does is pleasing to God. However, its right to rule comes from God. As such, *to resist* government is to *oppose* God and to prompt *condemnation*—divine judgment.

13:3-4. Paul also sees the noble purposes of government as reasons why to submit. First, government is *a minister of God for good.* Government is designed for our good to establish social welfare, domestic tranquility, etc. Without government, society would degenerate into chaos. The only law would be the law of the jungle. Clearly, any government is better than anarchy. Second, government is *a minister of God an avenger who brings wrath*. Government is also designed to punish evil doers and thus protect and secure justice for its citizens. The terms, *avenger* and *evil*, are also found in Rom. 12:17-21 where Paul prohibits acts of personal retribution and suggests that retribution is God's domain. God has clearly delegated part of this domain to government. It wields a *sword* of vengeance. Does this authority include capital punishment? I think so. Israel was given this authority (Ex 21:12-29).

13:5. Paul summarizes his reasons. Since government is designed for our good and is ordained by God, we should submit *for conscience sake*. Since government is designed to punish evil, we should submit *because of wrath*.

13:6-7. Paul concludes with some practical ways to submit to government. The first is to *pay taxes*. These taxes are designed to support the work of government and pay for the services of government officials. We should financially support *rulers* since they are *servants of God, devoting themselves* to their work. Paul broadens the idea to include our attitudes toward these officials. Not only should we behave properly toward government, but we should also have a proper attitude, respecting and reverencing rulers. We are to *fear* and *honor* them. To fear is to have appropriate respect for their office. This will lead to honoring them for their work. Paul leaves no room for disrespect even for corrupt officials. Paul modeled this respect in his trial before the Sanhedrin. There he apologized for his inappropriate response to Ananias, the High Priest, which he spoke unaware that he was high priest. He made it clear that it was inappropriate to speak against your rulers (Acts 23:2-5).

Love as Neighbors   *13:8-10*

[8]Owe nothing to anyone except to love one another; for he who loves his neighbor has fulfilled the law. [9]For this, "You shall not commit adultery, You shall not murder, You shall not steal, You shall not covet," and if there is any other commandment, it is summed up in this saying, "You shall love your neighbor as yourself." [10]Love does no wrong to a neighbor; therefore love is the fulfillment of the law.

Summary   Always sense a debt of love to each other; for love is the ultimate fulfillment of the Law.

Structural Layout

Owe nothing but to love one another.
    For
            He who loves has fulfilled the Law
            For
                    It is summed up: Love your neighbor
                    Love does no wrong to a neighbor
        Therefore
        Love is the fulfillment of the Law.

13:8-10 Commentary

Paul begins with the command to *love one another* (Rom. 13:8a) and then explains why (Rom. 13:8b-10). To love your neighbor is to fulfill the Law. The object of this love is one another, suggesting that the section is dealing with our relationships within the Church. However, he also broadens the object of our love by talking about loving our neighbors. So, there may be a more general object of this love.

It is also clear that Paul wants to establish the relationship between love and Law. Love is the fulfillment of the Law (Rom. 13:8, Rom. 13:10) and thus establishes a moral obligation for Christians even though they are no longer under the Law (Rom. 7:4).

13:8a. Paul introduces the exhortation to love one another with the prohibition, *owe nothing to anyone.* Does this mean that borrowing is wrong? No. Borrowing was a common practice (Ex. 22:14; 2 Kg. 14:3, 16:5; Mtt. 5:42). However, the Old Testament forbids charging interest to Jewish brethren (Ex. 22:25) for personal gain at the expense of the poor. Charging interest to foreigners was acceptable (Deut. 23:30). Paul's point is that we should never be in a position where we cannot pay back our debts. Those who borrow and do not repay are considered wicked (Ps. 37:21). However, Paul point is not to discuss debt but love.

There is one thing to which we are obligated. To *love one another* is one debt that we can never repay. As in Rom. 12:9, this love is *agape* love, a love of choice, a decision. The object of our love is *one another*. This is most probably a reference to the Christian community and therefore reflects back to Rom. 12:9-13. However, the following reference to loving your neighbor may suggest a broadening of the object to society in general. This would explain the location of the section between the prior section dealing with submission to government and the following command dealing with holy living.

13:8b-10. Paul explains why we should love one another. *He who loves his neighbor has fulfilled the law.* This teaching comes directly from the Lord (Matt. 22:39-40). Love should be the central principle that governs all human relationships. All prescriptive laws are based on love and find their fulfillment in love. Law is *summed up* in love. Love is the governing principle and individual laws are the application of the principle to a specific situation. Thus, it is essential that human relationships be based on internal love (Lev. 19:18) and not just on external commandments. There are many ways that love should be implemented that go beyond specific commandments. For instance, in Rom. 14:15 Paul suggests that eating food that results in harming a brother is a violation of love. Yet, there is no commandment against eating food that might offend or someway spiritual harm my brother. So, love is the ultimate fulfillment of law and goes beyond it.

Live Separated Lives   *13:11-14*

¹¹Do this, knowing the time, that it is already the hour for you to awaken from sleep; for now salvation is nearer to us than when we believed. ¹²The night is almost gone, and the day is near.

Therefore let us lay aside the deeds of darkness and put on the armor of light. ¹³Let us behave properly as in the day, not in carousing and drunkenness, not in sexual promiscuity and sensuality, not in strife and jealousy. ¹⁴But put on the Lord Jesus Christ, and make no provision for the flesh in regard to its lusts.

Summary The closeness of Christ's return should motivate us to live separate from the world, and in conformity to Christ.

Structural Layout

> This do, knowing the time
> > hour to awaken
> > salvation is nearer
> > night is almost gone, day is at hand
>
> Therefore
> > lay aside deeds of darkness
> > put on armor of light
> > behave properly as in the day
> > > not carousing, drunken, sexual promiscuity, strife
> >
> > put on the Lord Jesus Christ

13:11-14 Commentary

In this section Paul uses the second coming of Christ to motivate Christians to live morally consecrated lives. He begins with the motivation (Rom. 13:11-12a). Knowing how close we are to Christ's return and our ultimate salvation should cause us to act. He follows this with commands for change (Rom. 13:12b-14). We should abandon the past life of sin and take hold of our live in Christ.

13:11-12a. Paul beings with the words, *And this*. Our versions fill in what seems to be a missing imperative, *do*. *This* seems to look backward rather than forward and thus must refer either to the prior section about love (Rom. 13:8-10) or all the exhortation so far (Rom. 12:1-13:10). Though the pronoun is singular, it seems more likely that Paul is offering the motivation for performing all of the exhortations so far, rather than only the prior exhortation.

The motivation is in *knowing the time*. It is the time of *salvation*. Salvation has past, present and future aspects. Here it refers to the future, to final and complete deliverance from sin's power and consequences (Rom. 5:9-10). This future salvation will occur when Christ returns for His Church. This event is *at hand*, that is, it is imminent. It could occur at any time. This is the source of our motivation.

The past life of sin is pictured as the *night*. The future life, inaugurated by Christ's coming, is pictured as the *day*. We currently live in the dawning for the *night is almost gone, and the day is near*. Soon the sun will rise; Christ will come. This should motivate us to live in moral purity.

13:12b-14. In response, we should abandon the past and take hold of the future. The verbs, *lay aside* and *put on*, are in the aorist tense to indicate actions that are to be done completely as momentary events. These are not processes, but simple choices of the will. The picture is that of taking off and putting on clothing. We are to remove *the deeds of darkness*, the sinful actions of the past and replace them with the *armor of light*, actions that are proper for heaven-bound saints.

Paul expands the exhortations in Rom. 13:13. To put on the armor of light is to *behave properly as in the day*. As it is today, the activities of the night were associated with inappropriate activities and the activities of the day were associated with more appropriate things. Yet, Paul has also associated the day with the coming age of righteousness. We should be living up to that age in the way we conduct our lives in this age. What follows is a vise list of nighttime sins. Similar lists are found in 1 Pet. 4:3 and Gal. 5:19-21. The sins are grouped into three pairs. The first two pairs speak of hedonistic activities often associated with Gentiles. The last pair, *strife and jealousy*, deals more with interpersonal relationships and may be addressed more directly to the situation of the church at Rome.

Paul concludes his exhortation by telling his readers to *put on Christ*. They are to think and act like Christ. What would Christ do in a given situation? How would Christ react? We are to wear Christ on the outside of our lives so that others might see Christ through us.

Accept One Another   *14:1-15:13*

Summary   Accept each other as Christ has accepted you, not judging each other, nor tempting each other with your liberty.

Structural Layout

> Accept the one who is weak
> Do not judge, regard not with contempt
> Determine not to put a stumbling block in brother's path
> Accept one another just as Christ accepted us

Overview

This section addresses a difference of opinion between two groups within the church at Rome. The first Paul labels as *weak*. Such individuals abstained from meats and wine and set aside certain days as special holy days (Rom. 14:2, Rom. 14:5, Rom. 14:21). They lacked the conviction to abandon their external rules (Rom. 14:1, 23). The second group Paul labels as *strong*. These individuals had no misgiving about participation in the activities forbidden by the weak (Rom. 14:2, Rom. 14:5, Rom. 14:22). It seems most likely that the problem was a socio-religious problem between the Jewish and Gentile elements in the church. This would explain Paul's weaving the Jewish-Gentile issue back into the text in Rom. 15:8-12. It would not have been easy for Jews to abandon their dietary and religious customs. However, there is no idea in the section that the issue was anything other than cultural since Paul champions the cause of these weak Jews. The weak do not seem to have made this an issue of salvation. Yet the difference of opinion had fostered division and had polarized the groups.

Paul's main admonition is to accept one another (Rom. 14:1, Rom. 15:7). The two groups needed to learn mutual toleration. The first section (Rom. 14:1-3) is addressed to both groups and provides the main admonition. The second section (Rom. 14:4-12) is addressed primarily to the weak, instructing them not to judge their stronger brothers. The third section (Rom. 14:13-23) is addressed to the strong, instructing them not to cause their weaker brothers to stumble. The final section (Rom. 15:1-13) concludes with a renewed appeal to unity and acceptance.

This passage should be compared with Paul's similar instruction in 1 Cor. 8-10. Both passages deal with the weak and strong, both emphasize the responsibility of the strong to limit the use of their liberty, and both emphasize the importance of love.

Introductory Exhortation: Accept One Another   14:1-3

¹Now accept the one who is weak in faith, but not for the purpose of passing judgment on his opinions. ²One person has faith that he may eat all things, but he who is weak eats vegetables only. ³The one who eats is not to regard with contempt the one who does not eat, and the one who does not eat is not to judge the one who eats, for God has accepted him.

Summary   Accept one another, you who being weak in faith not judging the strong, and you who are strong in faith, not regarding the weak with contempt.

Structural Layout

Accept the one who is weak in faith, not for passing judgment
One has faith...eats all things   let him not regard with contempt
One is weak...eats vegetables only   let him not judge

14:1-3 Commentary

14:1. Paul begins with the main instruction *accept the one who is weak in faith*. The fact that this was addressed to the whole congregation suggests that those who were weak formed a small minority in the church. Accept can mean to take as a companion, to take into one's home with the collateral idea of kindness, or to grant one access to one's heart. The latter idea seems best here since our reception of others is to be modeled after Christ's reception of us (Rom. 15:7). As such, this reception must not lead to quarrelsome debates, *passing judgment on his opinions*. Our purpose is not to convince others of our position but to accept others in spite of their differing opinions. What Paul requests is mutual toleration and loving acceptance in areas that are non-essential or non-doctrinal. However, Paul did not tolerate heresy. Those who adhere to doctrinal error must be rejected (Rom. 16:17-20).

14:2. Next, Paul outlines the areas of disagreement. The strong Christian *has faith that he may eat all things*. That is, he has inner confidence about his liberty in Christ (Rom. 14:5, Rom. 14:22). This is not simply head knowledge but a dynamic confidence that strengthens the conscience (1 Cor. 8:7). Such individuals exhibit greater freedom in their actions. The weak Christian *eats vegetables only*. He is aware of liberty in Christ but continue to live under certain rules and restrictions because he lacks the confidence that formerly forbidden activities are now acceptable. If this person was to participate in these things, his conscience would be defiled by his lack of faith (Rom. 14:23, 1 Cor. 8:12). Paul does not view the weak as less spiritual. He never rebukes him for his weaknesses, nor does he ever instruct him to become strong. It seems that this is not an issue of spirituality, but of cultural conditioning (1 Cor.8:7).

14:3. Paul develops his instruction by describing what mutual toleration does not include. First, the strong must not *regard with contempt* the weak. The verb means to reject with great contempt (Luke 18:9, Acts 4:11). Those who appropriate their freedom in Christ most often regard with contempt those who lack their freedom. Second, the weak must not *judge* the strong. This judgment occurs when the weak attempts to apply his rules to the strong, assuming that his rules are divinely established. He must understand that his rules only guard his weak conscience. They are not required biblical standards.

Do Not Judge Your Brother 14:4-12

⁴*Who are you to judge the servant of another? To his own master he stands or falls; and he will stand, for the Lord is able to make him stand.*

⁵*One person regards one day above another, another regards every day alike. Each person must be fully convinced in his own mind. ⁶He who observes the day, observes it for the Lord, and he who eats, does so for the Lord, for he gives thanks to God; and he who eats not, for the Lord he does not eat, and gives thanks to God. ⁷For not one of us lives for himself, and not one dies for himself; ⁸for if we live, we live for the Lord, or if we die, we die for the Lord; therefore whether we live or die, we are the Lord's.*

⁹*For to this end Christ died and lived again, that He might be Lord both of the dead and of the living.*

¹⁰*But you, why do you judge your brother? Or you again, why do you regard your brother with contempt? For we will all stand before the judgment seat of God.* ¹¹*For it is written, "As I live, says the Lord, every knee shall bow to Me, And every tongue shall give praise to God."* ¹²*So then each one of us will give an account of himself to God.*

Summary   Do not judge your brother, God's servant, since God is judge, to whom each of us will give an account for our actions and motives.

Structural Layout

Who are you to judge another man's servant?
    Let each man be fully convinced.
    For the Lord (5 times)
But why do you judge your brother?
    We shall all stand before judgment seat of God.
    Each one will give an account.

14:4-12 Commentary

Paul addresses this section mainly to the weak, whose mistake is in judging the strong (Rom. 14:3b), though the strong are also included (Rom. 14:10) since they are the ones who express contempt. Paul's purpose is to rebuke them for judging their brothers. Paul structures the reprove in the form of rhetorical questions at the beginning and end of the section (Rom. 14:4, Rom. 14:10). The questions are followed by an explanation (Rom. 14:4b-9, Rom. 14:10b-12). The explanation is designed to explain that judgment is God's right, and to encourage personal self-evaluation of our actions.

14:4. Paul begins his rebuke with the question, *Who are you to judge the servant of another?* Paul returns to his diatribe style, using *you* in the singular (Rom. 14:10, Rom. 14:15, Rom. 14:20, Rom. 14:21, Rom. 14:22) with rhetorical questions. However, here he is addressing the Roman Christians, or at least a subset of them. They needed to understand that their judging was inappropriate since believers are the Lord's *servants*. He alone has the right to judge them since He is their *Master, kurios.* Paul must be referring to Christ since he identifies Christ as the Lord— *kurios* in Rom. 4:9. No judgment on the part of others will have any effect; *to his own master he stands or falls.*

14:5-9. Since God alone will judge his servants, those servants should be concerned about how their own actions will be judged by Him rather than being concerned about judging the actions of others. When God judges, the believer will be personally and individually evaluated for his own actions (14:12; 1 Cor. 3:8). Therefore, rather than being preoccupied with his brother's actions, he *must be fully convinced in his own minds* about his own actions. He will be judged not only on the basis of what he does, but also on the basis of his motives for doing it. In areas of Christian liberty, the Christian is free to choose. But the basis of that choice is important. He should be deciding based on what brings the greatest glory to the Lord. His actions should be *for the Lord* not for *himself.* He is the servant of Christ; he is not his own master (Rom. 6:22). *Christ died and lived again, that He might be Lord both of the dead and of the living.* The thought echoes the thought expressed by Paul in 1 Cor. 10:31. We have been bought with a price. All we do should be to the glory of God.

14:10-12. Paul echoes his rebuke with two more rhetorical questions. The second expands the rebuke to the strong, *why do you regard your brother with contempt.* He then repeats his instruction about the Lord's judgment. *We will all stand before the judgment seat of God.* This judgment of believers will occur when Christ returns to rapture the Church. The judgment will take place at the judgment seat (*bema*) of God. The bema was the official seat upon which the judge would sit to judge a case (Acts 18:16-17, Acts 25:6-10). The judgment seat of Christ is the place where Christians will be evaluated for the receiving of rewards (1 Cor. 3:10-15).

Does this instruction suggest that all judgment of Christians by other Christians is wrong? No. Note that in 1 Cor. 5:3 Paul severely judges an individual who is living in incest. In fact, Paul rebukes the church for not having judged the individual sooner. The difference is two-fold. First, in this passage the weaker brother is holding out his conscience as a personal standard for evaluating others. Paul held out the authoritative standard of the Word of God. Second, Paul's judgment was expressed in the context of church discipline. Here the judgment is individual. Unfortunately, Christians tend to judge others when they should not, and fail to judge them when they should.

Do Not Cause Your Brother to Stumble   14:13-23

[13]*Therefore let us not judge one another anymore, but rather determine this—not to put an obstacle or a stumbling block in a brother's way.*

[14]*I know and am convinced in the Lord Jesus that nothing is unclean in itself; but to him who thinks anything to be unclean, to him it is unclean.*

[15]*For if because of food your brother is hurt, you are no longer walking according to love. Do not destroy with your food him for whom Christ died.* [16]*Therefore do not let what is for you a good thing be spoken of as evil;* [17]*for the kingdom of God is not eating and drinking, but righteousness and peace and joy in the Holy Spirit.* [18]*For he who in this way serves Christ is acceptable to God and approved by men.*

[19]*So then let us pursue the things which make for peace and the building up of one another.* [20]*Do not tear down the work of God for the sake of food. All things indeed are clean, but they are evil for the man who eats and gives offense.* [21]*It is good not to eat meat or to drink wine, or to do anything by which your brother stumbles.* [22]*The faith which you have, have as your own conviction before God. Happy is he who does not condemn himself in what he approves.* [23]*But he who doubts is condemned if he eats, because his eating is not from faith; and whatever is not from faith is sin.*

Summary Do not bring harm to your brother by your actions, but rather limit your actions to build up your brother.

Structural Layout

> ¹³Therefore
>> determine not to put an obstacle or a stumbling block in a brother's way.
>>> ¹⁴nothing is unclean in itself;
>>> but to him who thinks anything to be unclean, to him it is unclean.
>> ¹⁵For
>>>> if because of food your brother is hurt,
>>> you are no longer walking according to love.
>> Do not destroy with your food him for whom Christ died.
> ¹⁶Therefore
>> do not let what is for you a good thing be spoken of as evil;
>>> ¹⁷for
>>>> the kingdom is not eating and drinking,
>>>> but righteousness and peace and joy in the Holy Spirit.
>>> ¹⁸For
>>>> he who in this serves Christ is acceptable to God, approved by

men.
> ¹⁹So then
>> let us pursue the things which make for peace
>>>> and the building up of one another.
> ²⁰Do not tear down the work of God for the sake of food.
>> All things indeed are clean,
>> but they are evil for the man who eats and gives offense.
> ²¹It is good not to eat meat or to drink wine,
>>> or *to do anything* by which your brother stumbles.

14:13-23 Commentary

Paul now turns his attention to the strong brother. He must be cautious in his use of his liberty, lest he causes the weaker brother to stumble (Rom. 14:13). The section is organized around several interrelated commands and clarifying statements. The use of *you* singular continues to the end of the chapter (Rom. 14:15, Rom. 14:20, Rom. 4:21, Rom. 14:22). Some have seen a chiastic structure as follows:

> stumbling block
>> nothing unclean but
>>> do not destroy
>>>> so then pursue peace
>>> do not tear down
>> all are clean but
> brother stumbles

It is difficult to know if this is intentional or not. The connective, *so then* at Rom. 14:19 suggests it is intentional but the additional material does not fit so nicely. What is clear is that Paul supports his instruction with reasons that probe deeply into the nature of human perception and divine importance. We must be conscious of these things as we consider how to decide on our activities within the family of faith. We see then two subsections, Rom. 14:13-18 and Rom. 14:20-23, which essentially deal with the same material. Rom. 14:19 is the conclusion and functions as the hinge of the chiasmus.

14:13-18. *Therefore* signals both a summary of Paul's command in Rom. 14:4-12 and a transition to a new command. Paul uses a play on word when he states, *let us not judge one another anymore, but rather determine this*. Both judge and determine translate the Greek word, *krinō*. With it Paul calls for a second type of self-evaluation. Not only should we determine if our actions are beneficial to the Lord (Rom. 14:6), but we should determine if our actions are harmful to our brother.

We must determine *not to put an obstacle or a stumbling block in a brother's way*. A *stumbling block* refers to the insensitive use of liberty resulting in the weaker brother performing the same acts when he does not have the faith to do so (1 Cor. 8:8-12). The result is not simply that the weak brother is offended, but that the weak are deeply harmed spiritually. They are *hurt* and *destroyed*. Paul calls such actions sin (1 Cor. 8:12).

Paul offers several reasons and explanations for the command. First, he gives a principle of moral relativism (Rom. 14:14). Good things, to the one who perceives them to be *unclean*, impure or profane, are indeed unclean. In this instance, perception, not essence, defines reality. Paul does not suggest the opposite, namely that evil things when perceived as good are good. Second, he states that such an act is unloving (Rom. 14:15). *You are no longer walking according to love* since it results in great harm. This lack of love is contrasted with Christ's loving sacrifice. *Do not destroy with your food him for whom Christ died.* When we cause a brother to stumble, we place greater value on our liberty than we do on our brother. Third, Paul suggests that such actions will destroy our own testimony (Rom. 14:16). People *rightly speak evil of* us because we have destroyed our weaker brother. Fourth, Paul explains that *the kingdom of God* has nothing to do with exercising our liberties but rather has everything to do with godly social relationships, *righteousness and joy and peace* (Rom. 14:17). Finally, he indicates that limiting our rights for the sake of others results in both divine and human favor (Rom. 14:18). We are both *acceptable to God and approved by men.*

14:19 *So then* marks a conclusion to the main exhortation and is the hinge of the chiasmus. We are to *pursue the things which make for peace.* Our actions should result in peace within the community of faith. Paul has already mentioned that this is an essential characteristic to the kingdom (Rom. 14:17). The opposite is strife and jealousy (Rom. 13:13).

Our actions should also result in *the building up of one another.* The noun, *oikodomē*, is also found in Rom. 15:2 where it is translated, *edification.* We should be vitally concerned about whether our actions will bring spiritual profit to others. The opposite is to hurt, destroy, and tear down our brothers by encouraging them to sin by doing what they do not have the faith to do (Rom. 14:23).

14:20-23. Paul begins his reiteration of his instruction by contrasting the work of God with food. *Do not tear down the work of God for the sake of food.* The *work of God* refers to your weaker brother. *Food* represents the exercising of one's liberty. Again, Paul offers a reason and explanation for the command. He suggests that such actions are *evil. All things indeed are clean, but they are evil for the man who eats and gives offense.* The evil is not innate within the food since *all things are clean.* Paul is not suggesting that all actions are morally pure. Indeed, many actions are sinful and disobedient. Paul speaks about things, like *food*, that are morally neutral or might even be considered good. When the exercise of such liberty has negative results, that liberty becomes *evil.* That to *give offense* is equal to causing someone to stumble is clear from the next parallel statement. *It is good not to eat meat or to drink wine, or to do anything by which your brother stumbles.* Instead Paul suggests that you keep your personal conviction about the action private. *The faith which you have, have as your own conviction before God.* This will result in far more happiness for you. *Happy is*

177

he who does not condemn himself. On the contrary, if you exercise your liberty, you will lead your weaker brother to sin because *his eating is not from faith; and whatever is not from faith is sin.* Paul ends with a principle of faith. Faith defines whether or not doing something debatable is sin. We must walk by faith.

Concluding Appeal to Unity   15:1-13

[1]Now we who are strong ought to bear the weaknesses of those without strength and not just please ourselves. [2]Each of us is to please his neighbor for his good, to his edification. [3]For even Christ did not please Himself; but as it is written, "The reproaches of those who reproached You fell on Me." [4]For whatever was written in earlier times was written for our instruction, so that through perseverance and the encouragement of the Scriptures we might have hope.

[5]Now may the God who gives perseverance and encouragement grant you to be of the same mind with one another according to Christ Jesus, [6]so that with one accord you may with one voice glorify the God and Father of our Lord Jesus Christ. [7]Therefore, accept one another, just as Christ also accepted us to the glory of God. [8]For I say that Christ has become a servant to the circumcision on behalf of the truth of God to confirm the promises given to the fathers, [9]and for the Gentiles to glorify God for His mercy; as it is written, "Therefore I will give praise to You among the Gentiles, And I will sing to Your name." [10]Again he says, "Rejoice, O Gentiles, with His people." [11]And again, "Praise the Lord all you Gentiles, And let all the peoples praise Him." [12]Again Isaiah says, "There shall come the root of Jesse, And He who arises to rule over the Gentiles, In Him shall the Gentiles hope." [13]Now may the God of hope fill you with all joy and peace in believing, so that you will abound in hope by the power of the Holy Spirit.

Summary With true unity, accept each other as Christ has accepted you.

Structural Layout

Now
>> may God grant you to be of the same mind
>>> with one accord
>>> with one voice
>>> according to Christ

> Wherefore
>> accept one another
>>> just as Christ accepted us
>>>> Servant: to circumcision and for the Gentiles

Now
>> may God fill you with joy, peace, hope

15:1-13 Commentary

The structure and purpose of Rom. 15:1-13 is difficult to analyze. Rom. 15:1-4 seem to continue Paul's advice to the strong Christian, yet there are clear differences. Paul substitutes *weaknesses of those without strength* for *weak* brothers; introduces a new verb, *please, areskō*; and adds the example of Christ. This example is developed throughout the passage. So, it seems that a break does occur at Rom. 15:1 and that this break marks the conclusion to the discourse begun at Rom. 14:1. Paul also uses verbs in the optative mood to introduce a prayer in Rom. 15:5 and Rom. 15:13. This is a stylistic inclusio that presents the closing in the form of a benediction (Rom. 15:5-13). The benediction begins with a prayer (Rom. 15:5-6) which is again picked up in Rom. 15:13. Between the two parts of the benediction Paul repeats the main exhortation (Rom. 15:7, Rom. 14:1) and offers a doctrinal reason for adhering to that exhortation (Rom. 15:8-12).

15:1-4. Paul begins his conclusion by reiterating his instruction to the strong. They must *bear the weaknesses of those without strength*. Paul places the major responsibility upon the strong. They must *bear* the burden. Why are the weak not instructed to become strong? The answer lies in the conscience. Since their conscience has been programmed over time (1 Cor. 8:7), it will take time to adjust it and gain the confidence necessary to do those things that they once considered sinful. In the meantime, the strong must bear the *weaknesses* of the weak. These weaknesses in conscience result in the rules and

179

regulations of the weak. The strong must be willing to live under these restrictions. The opposite is to *just please ourselves*. This selfish attitude is the opposite of love. He who loves considers his *neighbor* (Rom. 13:8-10) for his *edification* (1 Cor .8:1). Christ is now offered as the ultimate example of such love. He *did not please himself*. He took on our *reproaches* (Ps. 69:9). In the same way, we are to take on the weaknesses of the weak. Paul understands the Old Testament as a source of *instruction*. Psalm 69:9, not only teaches us about the sufferings of Messiah, but also provides a lesson for us to obey (1 Cor. 10:11, 2 Tim. 3:16-17). He also sees the Old Testament as a source of *hope*. Paul has spoken of hope only in the context of difficult situations— tribulation (Rom. 5:2-5, Rom. 8:20-24, Rom. 12:12) and barrenness (Rom. 4:18). Why speak of hope in this context? Possibly because as Christ needed to suffer under the *reproaches* of sin, so the strong must suffer under the *weaknesses* of the weak. Paul returns to this hope in Rom. 15:12-13.

15:5-6. Paul uses a verb in the optative mood to introduce his concluding prayer. The prayer emphasizes unity with the words, *same mind, one accord*, and *one voice*. Such unity is *according to Christ*. It is in harmony with the example of Christ seen throughout the passage (Rom. 15:3, Rom. 15:5, Rom. 15:7, Rom. 15:8). This unity is not simply conformity on the outside but is *one accord*— an internalized unity of soul. It leads us to *glorify God*. This praise to God becomes a major theme of Rom. 15:7-12

15:7-12. The connective, *therefore*, marks the final conclusion and echoes the thought of Rom. 14:1, *accept one another*. Paul offers Christ as both the example and the rationale for such acceptance. In explaining this Paul returns to the logical style found in chapters 1-11. Christ is *servant* both to the Jews and to the Gentiles (Rom. 15:8-9). His ministry to the Jews was to *confirm the promises* to Israel. This summarizes much of the material in Rom. 11. His ministry to *the Gentiles* results in their praise for *His mercy*. Paul ends the section with several Old Testament quotes. The phrases, *among the Gentiles*, *with His people*, and *all His peoples*, emphasize the unity and harmony that should exist between the two groups. The words, *praise* and *rejoice* emphasize that they should glorify God together.

15:13. Paul ends the section by returning to the benediction begun at 15:6. Paul prays for the qualities that are associated with unity: *joy* and *peace* (Rom. 14:17). These he associates with *hope*. Where there is joy and peace within the community of faith, there will also be great hope.

Epistolary Closing   *15:14-16:27*

Summary   Paul reviews his personal plans, requests prayer for himself, and sends closing greetings.

Structural Layout

> I have a longing to come to you
> > whenever I go to Spain to be helped on my way there
>
> Now I am going to Jerusalem
>
> Greet…
>
> Keep your eye on those
> > who cause dissensions
>
> Timothy…greet you
>
> Now to only wise God be glory forever. Amen.

Overview

The epistle closes much like the normal closing of a Greco-Roman letter. First, there is a section of personal remarks in which the writer communicates his plans and provides personal requests (Rom. 14:14-33). This is followed by personal greetings (Rom. 16:1-16), greetings from others (Rom. 16:21-24), and a closing salutation (Rom. 16:25-27). Paul also includes a short final word of admonition (Rom. 16:17-20).

Paul's Personal Plans   *15:14-33*

[14] And concerning you, my brethren, I myself also am convinced that you yourselves are full of goodness, filled with all knowledge and able also to admonish one another. [15] But

I have written very boldly to you on some points so as to remind you again, because of the grace that was given me from God, [10]to be a minister of Christ Jesus to the Gentiles, ministering as a priest the gospel of God, so that my offering of the Gentiles may become acceptable, sanctified by the Holy Spirit. [17]Therefore in Christ Jesus I have found reason for boasting in things pertaining to God. [18]For I will not presume to speak of anything except what Christ has accomplished through me, resulting in the obedience of the Gentiles by word and deed, [19]in the power of signs and wonders, in the power of the Spirit; so that from Jerusalem and round about as far as Illyricum I have fully preached the gospel of Christ. [20]And thus I aspired to preach the gospel, not where Christ was already named, so that I would not build on another man's foundation; [21]but as it is written, "THEY WHO HAD NO NEWS OF HIM SHALL SEE, AND THEY WHO HAVE NOT HEARD SHALL UNDERSTAND."

[22]For this reason I have often been prevented from coming to you; [23]but now, with no further place for me in these regions, and since I have had for many years a longing to come to you [24]whenever I go to Spain—for I hope to see you in passing, and to be helped on my way there by you, when I have first enjoyed your company for a while— [25]but now, I am going to Jerusalem serving the saints. [26]For Macedonia and Achaia have been pleased to make a contribution for the poor among the saints in Jerusalem. [27]Yes, they were pleased to do so, and they are indebted to them. For, if the Gentiles have shared in their spiritual things, they are indebted to minister to them also in material things. [28]Therefore, when I have finished this, and have put my seal on this fruit of theirs, I will go on by way of you to Spain. [29]I know that when I come to you, I will come in the fullness of the blessing of Christ.

[30]Now I urge you, brethren, by our Lord Jesus Christ and by the love of the Spirit, to strive together with me in your prayers to God for me, [31]that I may be rescued from those who are disobedient in Judea, and that my service for Jerusalem may prove acceptable to the saints; [32]so that I may come to you in joy by the will of God and find refreshing rest in your company. [33]Now the God of peace be with you all. Amen.

Summary Paul, commissioned to preach to the Gentiles in the remotest parts of the world, requests that the Romans support him in a ministry in Spain and asks for their prayers as he journeys to Jerusalem.

182

Structural Layout

> I have written to remind you
>> minister of Christ to the Gentiles
>> I aspire to preach where Christ not already named
>
> For this reason
>> I have a longing to come to you
>>> whenever I go to Spain to be helped on my way there
>> Now I am going to Jerusalem
>
> Now I urge you
>> strive together with me in your prayers

15:14-33 Commentary

This section is divided into three parts: a review of Paul's ministry to the Gentiles (Rom. 15:14-21), a statement of his future plans and request for support (Rom. 15:22-29), and a request for prayer (Rom. 15:30-33).

15:14-21. The first section lays the ground work for Paul's request for support. He begins with words of confidence concerning them (Rom. 15:14-15). Next, he reminds them that he has been commissioned by God to be an apostle *to the Gentiles* (Rom. 15:16-17). Finally, he states that his ministry to the Gentiles is that of a pioneer missionary, establishing new works in areas where no work presently exists (Rom. 15:18-21). His goal was *to bring about the obedience of the Gentiles by word and deed.* Paul's wording is carefully designed to emphasize that grace does have as its goal obedience (Rom. 6:16). Yet, this obedience can only be the result of faith (Rom. 1:5, Rom. 16:26).

15:22-29. This leads into a discussion of Paul's future plans. His apostolic duties, the reason why he has not been able to come to them in the past, are coming to an end in Asia Minor and Greece (Rom. 15:22-23). From Paul's perspective, the church in these regions has been established. As a result, Paul now set his sights on a new virgin mission field, *Spain.* However, the distance from Syria to Spain demanded that he find another base of support. Paul saw Rome as that base. He could visit Rome and then be *helped by them* to reach Spain (Rom. 15:24, 28-29). There is however, one more duty that Paul must perform before making this journey. He must deliver a famine relief offering, collected by the *churches of Macedonia and Achaia*, to *Jerusalem* (Rom. 15:25-27). This offering is mentioned in several of Paul's letters (1 Cor. 16:1, 1 Cor. 16:9; 2 Cor. 8:1-9:15). Paul's mention of the offering and his trip to Jerusalem (Acts 19:21) places the time of the writing of Romans at the end of his third missionary journey, most likely while he was in Greece (Acts 20:1-3). It is traditionally suggested that he wrote Romans while at Corinth.

15:30-33. Paul ends his personal comments with a request for prayer concerning the trip to Jerusalem. Paul knew that the Jews in Jerusalem bitterly opposed him. He asks them to pray first for his protection from his enemies, that he might *be rescued from those who are disobedient in Judea*, then for his reception by the Church, that *my service for Jerusalem may prove acceptable to the saints*. He realized that the Judaizers were spreading false reports about him (Acts 21:20-21). His hope was that the relief offerings would demonstrate his commitment to his own people and to their customs. The fervency of the request, *strive together with me*. hints at his emotional state. He had already received warnings about the trip and is clearly greatly concerned (Acts 20:22-23).

Paul's Personal Greetings   *16:1-16*

[1] I commend to you our sister Phoebe, who is a servant of the church which is at Cenchrea; [2] that you receive her in the Lord in a manner worthy of the saints, and that you help her in whatever matter she may have need of you; for she herself has also been a helper of many, and of myself as well.

[3] Greet Prisca and Aquila, my fellow workers in Christ Jesus, [4] who for my life risked their own necks, to whom not only do I give thanks, but also all the churches of the Gentiles; [5] also greet the church that is in their house. Greet Epaenetus, my beloved, who is the first convert to Christ from Asia. [6] Greet Mary, who has worked hard for you. [7] Greet Andronicus and Junias, my kinsmen and my fellow prisoners, who are outstanding among the apostles, who also were in Christ before me. [8] Greet Ampliatus, my beloved in the Lord. [9] Greet Urbanus, our fellow worker in Christ, and Stachys

my beloved. ^{10}*Greet Apelles, the approved in Christ. Greet those who are of the household of Aristobulus.* ^{11}*Greet Herodion, my kinsman. Greet those of the household of Narcissus, who are in the Lord.* ^{12}*Greet Tryphaena and Tryphosa, workers in the Lord. Greet Persis the beloved, who has worked hard in the Lord.* ^{13}*Greet Rufus, a choice man in the Lord, also his mother and mine.* ^{14}*Greet Asyncritus, Phlegon, Hermes, Patrobas, Hermas and the brethren with them.* ^{15}*Greet Philologus and Julia, Nereus and his sister, and Olympas, and all the saints who are with them.* ^{16}*Greet one another with a holy kiss. All the churches of Christ greet you.*

Summary   Paul greets many of his friends and co-workers who are at Rome.

Structural Layout

> I commend to you Phoebe
>> Our sister, servant of the church at Cenchrea

> Greet
>> Prisca and Aquila, Epaenetus, Mary, Andronicus and Junias, Ampliatus
>> Urbanus, Stachys, Apelles, the *household* of Aristobulus, Herodion
>> the *household* of Narcissus, Tryphaena and Tryphosa, Persis, Rufus
>> Asyncritus, Phlegon, Hermes, Patrobas, Hermas and the brethren
>> with them, Philologus and Julia, Nereus and his sister, and Olympas,
>> and all the saints who are with them,

> Greet one another with a holy kiss.

> All the churches of Christ greet you.

16:1-16 Commentary

The section is divided into two parts: a request for the church to receive Phoebe (16:1-2), and a long list of personal greetings (16:3-16).

16:1-2. In Paul's day, letters were generally personally delivered by a messenger (Col. 4:7; Eph. 6:21). *Phoebe* was the deliverer of the letter to the Romans. She was a *sister* in the Lord, a common title given to female believers. She was also a *servant of the church at Cenchrea.* Does the phrase refer to a recognized position in the church or merely to the generic sense of anyone who serves? The fact that a specific church is mentioned, and that she was the official carrier of the letter, lends support to the idea that she held a recognized position in the church. She is also called a *helper, prostatis*. This was can have a technical reference of patroness; or it can simply mean helper. If the more technical idea is correct, it lends even more weight to the idea that she had a recognized office, deaconess of the church (1 Tim.3:11, 1 Tim.5:3, 1 Tim.5:9).

16:3-16. The recommendation of Phoebe is joined with a list of greetings to various individuals at the church at Rome. In all 26 people are named and in addition several other individuals or groups are also greeted. This list indicates that, although Paul had never visited the church, he was thoroughly familiar with the church. Some of the greetings were to his coworkers (*Prisca and Aquila*, and *Urbanus*). Some were to Jewish believers (*Prisca and Aquila*, *Andronicus and Junias, Herodian, and Rufus*). Several women are in the listing (*Prisca, Junias*, Mary, *Narcissus, Tryphena, Tryphosa, Persis, Julia*, and *Nereus' sister*). One of the greetings is to a house church (Rom. 16:5). Though some have attempted to interpret *those who are of the household of Aristobulus* (Rom. 16:10) and *those of the household of Narcissus* (Rom. 16:11) as referring to house churches, it is more likely that these refer to families. All of the greetings are warm and complementary. Others were to well-known individuals with whom Paul has had many contacts.

Warning About The Judaizers   *16:17-20*

[17]Now I urge you, brethren, keep your eye on those who cause dissensions and hindrances contrary to the teaching which you learned, and turn away from them. [18]For such men are slaves, not of our Lord Christ but of their own appetites; and by their smooth and flattering speech they deceive the hearts of the unsuspecting. [19]For the report of your obedience has reached to all; therefore I am rejoicing over you, but I want you to be wise in what is good and innocent in what is evil. [20]The God of peace will soon crush Satan under your feet. The grace of our Lord Jesus be with you.

Summary   Beware of the deception of the Judaizers and reject them.

Structural Layout

> Keep your eye on those
> > who cause dissensions
> > > contrary to teaching you learned
>
> turn away from them
> > slaves not of Christ
> > deceive hearts of unsuspecting

16:17-20 Commentary

In this section Paul warns the church not to accept Judaizers *who cause dissensions and hindrances contrary to the teaching which you learned.* First, they were to be alert. *Keep your eye on* means to be continually vigilant. Heresy is subtle. It employs *smooth and flattering speech* that can *deceive the hearts of the unsuspecting.* It can quickly overcome those who are gullible (Jude 3-4). Second, he commands them to separate from these heretics. *Turn away from them.* When it comes to the truths of the Word, we must not be tolerant. Heresy must be withstood and rejected. Christians need wisdom to know when to be tolerant (Rom. 14:1) and when to be intolerant.

Greetings from Paul's Companions   *16:21-24*

²¹Timothy my fellow worker greets you, and so do Lucius and Jason and Sosipater, my kinsmen. ²²I, Tertius, who write this letter, greet you in the Lord. ²³Gaius, host to me and to the whole church, greets you. Erastus, the city treasurer greets you, and Quartus, the brother. ²⁴[The grace of our Lord Jesus Christ be with you all. Amen.]

Summary   Timothy, my traveling companions, and those here in Corinth send greetings.

Structural Layout

> Timothy, Lucius, Jason, Sosipater greet you
> Tertius greets you
> Gaius, Erastus, Quartus greet you

16:21-24 Commentary

This section begins with greetings from *Timothy, Lucius, Jason,* and *Sosipater.* Timothy, Paul's assistant from the time of the 2nd missionary journey (Act 16:1), and Sosipater (Sopater), a believer from Berea, are mentioned as traveling companions in Acts 20:4, who left Greece with Paul after writing Romans. Lucias, though Origen identified him with Luke, is unknown. Jason may possibly be the same Jason who was forced before the authorities in Thessalonica (Acts 17:5-9). *Tertius* was Paul's amanuensis, a person employed to write from either dictation or from notes. Since Romans exhibits Paul's style and vocabulary, it is more likely that Tertius simply wrote what was dictated. It was uncommon for the amanuensis to provide a personal greeting at the end of the letter. This may indicate that he was a Christian. *Gaius* is also mentioned as one of Paul's traveling companions in Acts 20:4 where he is associated with Derbe. However, here Paul calls him his *host*, which seems to suggest he was from Corinth. This is confirmed in 1 Cor.1:14. The problem can be resolved if we associate the phrase, *of Derbe*, with Timothy (Acts 16:1). *Erastus, the city treasurer* also sent greetings. It is possible that an early Latin inscription found at Corinth may refer to this individual. It reads, *'Erastus laid this pavement at his own expense, in appreciation of his appointment as aedile.'* It is likely that he was well-to-do and influential within the community. A greeting comes from *Quartus*, about which nothing is known except that he lived in Corinth.

Rom. 16:24 is missing from the earliest Greek manuscripts. The external testimony is so limited that it can be concluded with much certainty that the verse is not original.

Closing Doxology   *16:25-27*

[25]Now to Him who is able to establish you according to my gospel and the preaching of Jesus Christ, according to the revelation of the mystery which has been kept secret for long ages past, [26]but now is manifested, and by the Scriptures of the prophets, according to the commandment of the eternal God, has been made known to all the nations,

leading to obedience of faith; ²⁷to the only wise God, through Jesus Christ, be the glory forever. Amen.

Summary   Paul ends the letter with a final doxology of praise to God who establishes them according to the gospel leading to an obedience that is sourced in faith.

Structural Layout

<pre>
Now
     to Him
          who is able to establish you
               according to my gospel
                    and preaching of Jesus Christ
               according to revelation
                    of the mystery
                         kept secret,
                         now manifested
                              made known to all the nations
                         leading to obedience of faith

     to only wise God
          be glory forever.

Amen.
</pre>

16:25-27 Commentary

In this closing benediction Paul describes God in two ways. First, He is the God *who is able to establish you.* To establish is Paul's way of summarizing all that God does in providing a sure footing upon which to build your life. He has justified you in Christ and has prepared you for glory. He does all this *according to my gospel.* Paul began with the gospel (Rom. 1:16) and ends with the gospel. This gospel includes the *preaching of Jesus Christ.* Jesus is the object of the proclamation. He is the one who is central to the gospel (Rom. 1:3) and who has performed the work fundamental to this gospel (Rom. 3:24-25). Paul calls this truth a *mystery.* It was in the past kept secret but is now fully revealed. It leads to the *obedience of faith* (Rom. 1:5). This is obedience that is sourced in faith (Rom. 1:5, Rom. 15:18). True obedience to God can only be produced when we believe.

Second, God is *the only wise God.* This wonderful plan is the outworking of a wise God (Rom. 11:33); for no human could ever have devised a plan that would allow a holy God to forgive sinners. *Through Jesus Christ* God enacted such a plan. He alone deserves *the glory forever.*

Appendix A
Justification in Romans

In Romans 1-11 Paul uses several semantically related Greek words in his discussion of justification by faith. Unfortunately, these words are not all translated into English using the same semantic root. Yet, when we observe them in Greek, the semantic relationship is obvious. All of these words include the cognate root, *dikai-*. They include:

dikaioō	justify, declare righteous
dikaiōma	righteous deed, justification
dikaios	righteous, just
dikaiosunē	righteousness

These words occur in the following verses in Romans. All but one are found in the opening eleven chapters.

Rom. 1:17 For in it the righteousness of God is revealed from faith to faith; as it is written, "But the righteous man shall live by faith."

Rom. 2:5 But because of your stubbornness and unrepentant heart you are storing up wrath for yourself in the day of wrath and revelation of the righteous judgment of God,

Rom. 2:13 for it is not the hearers of the Law who are just before God, but the doers of the Law will be justified.

Rom. 3:4 May it never be! Rather, let God be found true, though every man be found a liar, as it is written, "That You may be justified in Your words, And prevail when You are judged."

Rom. 3:5 But if our unrighteousness demonstrates the righteousness of God, what shall we say? The God who inflicts wrath is not unrighteous, is He? (I am speaking in human terms.)

Rom. 3:10 as it is written, "There is none righteous, not even one;

191

Rom. 3:20	because by the works of the Law no flesh will be justified in His sight; for through the Law comes the knowledge of sin.
Rom. 3:21	But now apart from the Law the righteousness of God has been manifested, being witnessed by the Law and the Prophets,
Rom. 3:22	even the righteousness of God through faith in Jesus Christ for all those who believe; for there is no distinction;
Rom. 3:24	being justified as a gift by His grace through the redemption which is in Christ Jesus;
Rom. 3:25	whom God displayed publicly as a propitiation in His blood through faith. This was to demonstrate His righteousness, because in the forbearance of God He passed over the sins previously committed;
Rom. 3:26	for the demonstration, I say, of His righteousness at the present time, so that He would be just and the justifier of the one who has faith in Jesus.
Rom. 3:28	For we maintain that a man is justified by faith apart from works of the Law.
Rom. 3:30	since indeed God who will justify the circumcised by faith and the uncircumcised through faith is one.
Rom. 4:2	For if Abraham was justified by works, he has something to boast about, but not before God.
Rom. 4:3	For what does the Scripture say? "Abraham believed God, and it was credited to him as righteousness."
Rom. 4:5	But to the one who does not work, but believes in Him who justifies the ungodly, his faith is credited as righteousness,
Rom. 4:6	just as David also speaks of the blessing on the man to whom God credits righteousness apart from works:

Rom. 4:9   Is this blessing then on the circumcised, or on the uncircumcised also? For we say, "Faith was credited to Abraham as righteousness."

Rom. 4:11   and he received the sign of circumcision, a seal of the righteousness of the faith which he had while uncircumcised, so that he might be the father of all who believe without being circumcised, that righteousness might be credited to them,

Rom. 4:13   For the promise to Abraham or to his descendants that he would be heir of the world was not through the Law, but through the righteousness of faith.

Rom. 4:22   Therefore it was also credited to him as righteousness.

Rom. 4:25   He who was delivered over because of our transgressions, and was raised because of our justification.

Rom. 5:1   Therefore, having been justified by faith, we have peace with God through our Lord Jesus Christ,

Rom. 5:7   For one will hardly die for a righteous man; though perhaps for the good man someone would dare even to die.

Rom. 5:9   Much more then, having now been justified by His blood, we shall be saved from the wrath of God through Him.

Rom. 5:16   The gift is not like that which came through the one who sinned; for on the one hand the judgment arose from one transgression resulting in condemnation, but on the other hand the free gift arose from many transgressions resulting in justification.

Rom. 5:17   For if by the transgression of the one, death reigned through the one, much more those who receive the abundance of grace and of the gift of righteousness will reign in life through the One, Jesus Christ.

Rom. 5:18   So then as through one transgression there resulted condemnation to all men, even so through one act of righteousness there resulted justification of life to all men.

Rom. 5:19   For as through the one man's disobedience the many were made sinners, even so through the obedience of the One the many will be made righteous.

Rom. 5:21   so that, as sin reigned in death, even so grace would reign through righteousness to eternal life through Jesus Christ our Lord.

Rom. 6:13   and do not go on presenting the members of your body to sin as instruments of unrighteousness; but present yourselves to God as those alive from the dead, and your members as instruments of righteousness to God.

Rom. 6:16   Do you not know that when you present yourselves to someone as slaves for obedience, you are slaves of the one whom you obey, either of sin resulting in death, or of obedience resulting in righteousness?

Rom. 6:18   and having been freed from sin, you became slaves of righteousness.

Rom. 6:19   I am speaking in human terms because of the weakness of your flesh. For just as you presented your members as slaves to impurity and to lawlessness, resulting in further lawlessness, so now present your members as slaves to righteousness, resulting in sanctification.

Rom. 6:20   For when you were slaves of sin, you were free in regard to righteousness.

Rom. 7:12   So then, the Law is holy, and the commandment is holy and righteous and good.

Rom. 8:10   If Christ is in you, though the body is dead because of sin, yet the spirit is alive because of righteousness.

Rom. 8:30   and these whom He predestined, He also called; and these whom He called, He also justified; and these whom He justified, He also glorified.

Rom. 8:33   Who will bring a charge against God's elect? God is the one who justifies;

Rom. 9:30   What shall we say then? That Gentiles, who did not pursue righteousness, attained righteousness, even the righteousness which is by faith;

Rom. 9:31   but Israel, pursuing a law of righteousness, did not arrive at that law.

Rom. 10:3   For not knowing about God's righteousness and seeking to establish their own, they did not subject themselves to the righteousness of God.

Rom. 10:4   For Christ is the end of the law for righteousness to everyone who believes.

Rom. 10:5   For Moses writes that the man who practices the righteousness which is based on law shall live by that righteousness.

Rom. 10:6   But the righteousness based on faith speaks as follows: "Do not say in your heart, 'Who will ascend into heaven?' (that is, to bring Christ down),

Rom. 10:10   for with the heart a person believes, resulting in righteousness, and with the mouth he confesses, resulting in salvation.

Rom. 14:17   for the kingdom of God is not eating and drinking, but righteousness and peace and joy in the Holy Spirit.

Appendix B
The Aorist Tense

The following comments are commonly accepted by grammarians; however, Frank Stagg, in the article, "The Abused Aorist", The Journal of Biblical Literature, June, 1972, pp. 222-231, summarizes the findings. He makes two important observations.

1. The aorist tense does not indicate once-for-all action. When an action is done once, and once only, the context must indicate this through specific words and phrases (Heb. 10:10, 1 Pet. 3:18).

2. The aorist tense says nothing regarding the kind of action involved, it is undefined. The action is viewed without reference to duration, interruption, completion or anything else. The aorist can cover any kind of action: single or multiple, momentary or extended, broken or unbroken, completed or open-ended. The aorist simply refrains from describing.

Since the Greek aorist tense expresses nothing regarding the kind of action involved this can be derived only from the context. Aorist merely signifies that the action occurred, but does not describe the action. The context will help the exegete decide whether the action extended over a long period of time or was momentary. Such statements as "the aorist tense proves that this is once-for-all action" or "the aorist tense proves that someone yields once for all to God" are false. The context may indicate this, but the aorist says nothing regarding it. The term aorist means undefined. Stagg in his article feels that departure from the aorist is exegetically more significant than the presence of the aorist.

If this is true why do the grammars describe the aorist as punctiliar? The aorist is punctiliar in its statement—it says the action happened--nothing more. It does not necessarily describe punctiliar action. This is clear in

Jesus' statement "forty-six years was this temple in building" (Jn. 2:20), where the aorist tense is used. The term, *constative* aorist, also shows that the aorist does not describe punctiliar action only.

More recently D. A. Carson has echoed Stagg's observations. For additional study, consult his book, <u>Exegetical Fallacies</u>. Baker Books, 1996.

Made in the USA
Monee, IL
17 June 2021

71623983R00115